THE COMPLETE BOOK OF
CASINO POKER

◆

Gary Carson

LYLE STUART
Kensington Publishing Corp.
www.kensingtonbooks.com

LYLE STUART BOOKS are published by

Kensington Publishing Corp.
850 Third Avenue
New York, NY 10022

All Kensington titles, imprints and distributed lines are available at special quantity discounts for bulk purchases for sales promotions, premiums, fund-raising, educational, or institutional use. Special book excerpts or customized printings can also be created to fit specific needs. For details, write or phone the office of the Kensington special sales manager: Kensington Publishing Corp., 850 Third Avenue, New York, NY 10022, attn: Special Sales Department; phone 1-800-221-2647.

Lyle Stuart is a trademark of Kensington Publishing Corp.

First printing: November 2004

10 9 8 7 6 5 4 3 2 1

Printed in the United States of America

ISBN 0-8184-0638-0

CONTENTS

FOREWORD

If you're completely new to poker, this is probably not the book for you. I assume you already know the basics of the game—you know that a flush beats a straight and know the basic mechanics of checking, betting, raising, and folding. If you know these basics and have some experience playing on the kitchen table, then you're the intended audience for this book. This book is about the way poker is played in most of today's public cardrooms.

The introductory chapter outlines the book and introduces the key concepts of position, aggression, draws, and tells. The book is centered around the idea of selective aggression, and the introductory chapter shows how position, draws, and tells relate to aggression. Chapter 1 refers to some aspects of hold'em, Omaha, and stud that you might not be familiar with. If this is the case, don't worry about it, just come back to it after you've read the later chapters on these games.

Chapter 2 covers hold'em, the most popular poker game in most cardrooms. It is primarily a game of high cards and position. Position is fixed for each betting round, so the value of late position accumulates with each betting round.

Seven-card stud (chapter 3) was once the predominant poker game in the United States. It's still popular in the Northeast but is mostly only played at low limits in the Midwest and Western states. This book focuses on the most common cardroom version of seven-card stud: the low-limit, no-ante version.

Omaha (chapter 4), the high-only version, isn't widely spread in cardrooms, but it's popular in some locations. Also, I think that an understanding of some of the principles of Omaha (high only) helps you understand the more popular game of Omaha hi/lo split.

Hi/lo split games (chapter 5) aren't as common in cardrooms as other games. Cardrooms hesitate to offer the games because splitting the pot slows the game and reduces the rake. The fewer the hands, the smaller the drop. Online cardrooms do offer these games, since splitting a pot online doesn't require any additional time. When they are offered, they tend to be popular, particularly among loose players.

I devote chapter 6 to position. This chapter shows how position can affect hand values and the importance of the extra information gained from late position. When you are first to act, you know almost nothing about the strength of other players' hands or the odds you'll get from callers on the hand. Both of these pieces of information are critical in estimating the value of your hand. Late position also adds value to your hand by withholding information about the strength of your hand from opponents.

Selective aggression is the key to winning poker. By aggression, I mean betting and raising instead of checking and calling. The value gained by the deception of passive play with a strong hand is often less than the value gained by straightforward aggression. Good things happen to those who bet and chapter 7 illustrates this with examples. Betting forces others into making tough decisions, thereby increasing the chances of them making a mistake. It's those mistakes made by others that create your profit.

Aggression is often the best course even when you don't have the best hand—under most game conditions, aggression with the best draw pays large dividends. Chapter 8, which focuses on outs and draws, shows examples of how aggression with the best draw can pay off, sometimes in unexpected ways. You don't always need the best hand to have the best hand.

A tell is a player's behavior that gives you a clue to the strength of his hand. Chapter 9 gives examples of tells and shows how you can sometimes induce players to give off classic tells. The mantra for deciphering tells is "strong means weak." A player who is acting strong probably has a weak hand. But the word "acting" means just that—an act. Strong behavior that is natural, not an act, usually means a strong hand.

Game selection (chapter 10) is the key to winning at poker. Mistake-free poker isn't enough to ensure a win. It's not even necessary. What you need to ensure a win are opponents who are making more mistakes than you. Finding opponents who make mistakes you can profit from is what game selection is all about.

Tournaments are becoming increasingly popular, particularly with the recent television success of World Series of Poker broadcasts on ESPN and broadcasts of World Poker Tour events on the Travel Channel.

The small buy-in, weekday afternoon tournament doesn't play like the five-day finale event at the World Series of Poker. Chapter 11 discusses play of typical small buy-in, fast-paced events.

Most cardrooms these days run frequent promotions, ranging from bad beat jackpots that run into the tens of thousands of dollars to hourly drawings for free T-shirts. Chapter 12 focuses on these promotions and on how some of them should affect the way you play the game.

Chapter 13 discusses the universality of poker concepts to all forms of poker. It shows, as an example, how the concept of live cards in seven-card stud and the concept of domination in hold'em are really just different names for the basic concept of having a strong draw. This final chapter also shows how selective aggression is the key factor driving any fundamental strategic concept.

One of the things my previous book was criticized for is that I didn't give a taste of how much patience this all takes. So, I'm making sure this book does. It takes a lot of patience. The subtitle of an old poker book is *The Waiting Game* and that's an apt description of poker. Wait for the right situation. Then fire. But make sure the situation is right. If the situation is not right, then just wait, it will be soon.

ACKNOWLEDGMENTS

I owe a big debt to many of the posters on the Internet newsgroup rec.gambling.poker. Some of the particular posters I've benefited from over the years are Peg Smith, Alan Bostick, and Tad Perry.

I don't play a lot of Omaha high, so both my understanding of this game and chapter 4 benefited greatly from some posts on rec.gambling.poker by Barry Tannanbaum.

My chapter on seven-card card stud particularly benefited from various contributions to discussion threads by Linda Sherman and Ashley Adams (author of *Winning 7-Card Stud* [2003]).

The Omaha/8 part of chapter 5 benefited from discussions with Steve Badger, Ken Kubey, and Stephen Carbonara.

Chapter 9 benefited from some ideas on tells from various posters on rec.gambling.poker, in particular Lee Munzer and Paul Gennero.

Chapter 11 benefited from discussions with John Davis, Patri Friedman, John Hartzell, Grant Denn, and Paul McMullin, among others.

1

Introduction

CARDROOM POKER

In many ways, poker played in a cardroom differs from poker played over the kitchen table. It has more structure, some might even say rigidity. Cardroom poker tends to be fast paced and the players are often more serious minded. Usually, the other players expect you to make decisions quickly and act promptly. Cardroom games can be just as social as home games, but players in cardroom games do tend to take the game itself more seriously than do most home-game players.

Poker is a thinking game. It is not a game to play mindlessly unless you really just don't care about the money. This is especially true when your cardroom opponents are taking the game seriously. But thinking can be hard work and taking the game seriously isn't always easy to do. Until you spend some time playing in casino cardrooms, it can be a little frustrating to try and play both thoughtfully and quickly, all the while keeping up a social banter. Cardroom poker tends to be fast paced.

Some casino cardrooms aren't even cardrooms, they are just a few poker tables set amid a sea of clanging, ringing slot machines that provide constant distraction. Thought tends to take time and effort, sometimes a lot of effort. Sometimes, it seems impossible to concentrate. But it's what you have to do. Meaningful action is driven by thought and, over the long run, how you think determines whether you come out ahead in the game or end up stuck. Some of the best poker players also excel at other mental games such as chess, bridge, or even scrabble. Poker is an exciting blend of a gambling game and a mental exercise. It's a great game. But it's not an easy game if you intend to play to win.

Take your time. You don't have to let them rush you. And you certainly don't have to let them confuse you. Cardrooms have their own way of doing things. If you're uncertain about a rule or procedure, just stop and ask the dealer for an explanation.

Even though poker is probably the most popular card game in America, twenty years ago only three states had legal cardrooms. Today, public cardrooms are now in sixteen states and private poker games are legal in most states. The growth in the cardroom industry is creating a surge of new interest in poker.

Since this recent growth of the cardroom industry in the United States, procedural rules for the games commonly played in cardrooms have become fairly standardized. There's no central body that dictates procedures, and every cardroom does have its own idiosyncrasies, but cardrooms do tend to have many of the same procedures.

Hold'em, seven-card stud, and, to a lesser extent, Omaha and Omaha hi/lo split (8 or better) are the primary cardroom poker games spread. You'll sometimes find seven-card stud hi/lo split (8 or better). The rules for play in the standard games only have small differences between cardrooms. Some players still use the terms "Texas hold'em" and "Omaha hold'em" to distinguish between these two games. I don't do that—I just call the game when you get two cards and combine zero, one, or two of them with five, four, or three of the cards on the board hold'em and the game where you get four cards and combine two of them with three from the board Omaha.

This book covers the procedural aspects of these games, then delves into the important strategic concepts of poker. These concepts are common to all the games. Because it's the most popular and most common casino poker game, most of the examples I give involve hold'em. The book does, however, cover the basics of all the games typically found in cardrooms.

The strategic elements are organized around the central concepts of position, aggression, draws, and tells. I demonstrate these concepts through example by recounting poker hands I've encountered. Discussion of specific hands I've played serves as illustration of the principal concepts. I also include hands where I made mistakes. I think readers often learn better from the mistakes of others rather than trying to mimic someone who seems to play perfectly. Much of playing winning poker is simply avoiding mistakes while waiting for your opponents to make mistakes. The waiting part can sometimes be the most difficult. Chapter 14 gives a hint about how much patience is required to make all this work.

The organizing principle of the book is aggression, and I show how position, draws, and tells relate to selective aggression. There is also a discussion of hand domination and how the ideas related to domination fit into a selectively aggressive approach to the game.

I'm addressing somewhat of a dual market: a "second book" for the growing ranks of serious or semiserious poker players and an introduction to casino poker for those players new to casino poker but not new to poker. I assume the reader has played some poker and is familiar with the basics of the game. Basic strategy for games offered in today's cardrooms—hold'em, Omaha, Omaha hi/lo split (8 or better), seven-card stud, seven-card stud hi/lo split (8 or better)—is covered and I use specific examples to illustrate some of the fundamental concepts of winning poker, such as position and selective aggression, and how these concepts apply to the kind of loose game that confronts most poker players.

There are also many examples from hands played on online cardrooms. When appropriate, I point out some of the differences between online play and live play. But I only deal with the online differences incidentally, as I hope to dwell on the differences between online play and live play more fully in a future book.

CARDROOMS

Selecting a Cardroom

In some areas of the country, you will only have one cardroom. In other areas, you'll have a wide range of cardrooms within a short driving distance. You might feel more comfortable at a small cardroom, where you're likely to quickly become known by the staff and they'll be more likely to make you feel at home. Or you may prefer the choices in game selection offered by a larger cardroom. These preferences are a personal issue you have to decide for yourself.

Personally, I prefer rooms that are moderately sized, but not really large. I like the room to be large enough to have enough business so that I'm reasonably likely to find a game anytime I visit. Very small rooms often don't have games in the mornings, or very late at night, and have limited selection on most weeknights. But I think the very large rooms tend to attract more than their share of pros and hustlers, making the games tougher. Even though the bigger rooms often have more games to choose from, the midsized rooms seem to have more games full of weak players to choose from.

You'll find the same kind of situation among online cardrooms. You'll always be able to find a game in the larger, more popular sites. But you'll often be more likely to find a good game at the moderately popular sites.

Game Selection

The biggest mistake players make is to pigeonhole themselves as a player of a certain limit and game. "I'm a 5/10 hold'em player," they'll think of themselves. And they'll play 5/10 hold'em, even though the 3/6 hold'em game right next to them is a much better game. They'll never realize it because they'll never even look.

Simply put, a lot of players putting a lot of money in the pot makes for a good game. If there aren't a lot of players playing each hand in your game, and players aren't often calling raises cold in order to play, then you probably should be walking around the room to see if you can find a better game than the one you're in.

Game selection is the key to winning at poker. You don't win money at poker by being a good player. You win money by being a better player than the others at your table. Don't forget this. For this reason, it's important to learn all the games that are available to play. If you see a really good Omaha/8 game, you want to be able to play in it. You don't want to be shut out of the best game in the room because you only know how to play hold'em.

Learn how to play hold'em, seven-card stud, Omaha, and hi-lo split games. Don't be ashamed to play at a lower limit than you usually play at. The best game, the game with the most profit potential, isn't always the biggest game in the room.

Cardroom Procedures

When you enter a cardroom, you don't just walk around the room, find an empty seat, and sit down. You need to be seated by the floorman or, in a large cardroom, by a lower-level employee called the brush. Generally, there will be some sort of podium, or maybe just an employee with a clipboard. Approach the podium and ask the floor what games are being offered. He'll tell you the limits and games available. Some of them will have open seats available, some will have waiting lists for a seat.

If you are put on a waiting list, you'll be paged when your seat is available. Ask the floorman whether the page will carry to the casino area outside the cardroom. If so, you can wander around the casino while waiting for your seat. But if you're going to leave the area of the cardroom, make sure the floorman knows where you're going.

When you are seated, you'll have to buy chips. Some poker rooms have a cage to buy chips from. Some have chip runners who sell chips to customers. In some games, you just buy chips from the dealer. Usually, the floorman, or whichever employee is seating you, will get your chips for you. Simply ask what you need to do to get chips.

If you're playing seven-card stud, you'll be dealt a hand right away.

If you're playing hold'em or Omaha, you may need to post a third blind to get a hand right away. Either that or wait until it's your turn to post the big blind. I'll explain about blinds in more detail later. Some cardrooms don't require a new player to post. Just ask, and the dealer will tell you. Sometimes, the dealer will just deal you a hand assuming you intend to post. This can cause some conflict if you don't intend to post.

STRATEGIC CONCEPTS

There is no magical "poker strategy" that will lead you to riches. Consistently beating the game in the long run requires thought, discipline, and the ability to adapt to changing circumstances. A rigid application of a set of memorized rules won't get you very far. I can't stress this enough. Thinking about the game and about your actions is critical. Whatever it is you do, you need to have a solid reason for doing it and an expected outcome from doing it. Whether you actually win or lose a particular hand makes no difference at all. Just keep doing the right things and the winning and losing takes care of itself. Thinking "what can I do to win this pot?" is sometimes a good way of thinking, but more often it's the way to disaster. Winning money at poker is about making bets where you have the best of it, not winning pots.

Different situations call for thinking in terms of different strategic perspectives. This book won't give you a set of playing rules or a bag of tricks or ploys. Simple, straightforward play will get the money in most games. But straightforward doesn't mean mindless, repetitive actions. It means a clear relationship between what you do and a desired outcome. The ideas in this book are geared to most games—those loose, low-limit games populated by players who came to play. But it's up to you to adapt those ideas to whatever specific circumstance you find yourself in.

The primary tools that can guide your thinking come from

mathematics and psychology. The game will play itself out according to a mixture of mathematics and psychology. The situation determines the best mix of psychology and math to put into the analysis of that situation. You'll sometimes see a debate about which is more important: knowing the mathematics of the game or understanding the players. That is a nonissue. These two things aren't really separable. Knowing the players does you no good if you don't understand the mathematics. And if you don't know the players, you won't know how to use the mathematics.

This book is meant for beginners, but it's not an instruction manual for completely novice poker players. The intended audience is poker players with at least some experience, experienced enough to at least know the procedural rules of the game and how to play various poker variants. You need to know that a flush beats a straight to read this book to any benefit. However, I do think more advanced players can also profit from it.

Throughout the book, I present fundamental poker concepts and illustrate a concept with a particular hand. Most of the illustrations are from hold'em and the other typical casino games of seven-card stud, seven-card hi-lo/8, and Omaha hi-lo/8. Some examples also come from games such as five-card draw, razz (seven-card lowball), and even hold'em hi-lo/8

The core principle of this book is selective aggression. The primary guides to the selectivity of your aggression are the value that you get from position or from a draw and the information you get from position or a tell. Of course, these aren't the only reasons for aggression, as a poker buddy of mine likes to say, "I raise 'cause it's fun." Even though it's said as a joke, like all good jokes, it has a kernel of truth. Raising a lot does help make the game more fun, and if you're not going to be having fun, then there really isn't a point to be playing.

Aggression is the key to winning poker, but how you use aggression in the various forms of poker does vary somewhat. For example, in hold'em big pairs are key, while in Omaha hi/lo split it's draws that are of critical importance. Raising or betting is done for different reasons in different situations.

Aggression is the central concept in playing winning poker, but position is the key to selective aggression. Actually, position is the key to almost everything you do. Position is power. Position is information. By position, I usually mean the location of your seat relative to that of the first player to act. Every action you take needs to first be considered in light of your position. Hands that are unplayable from early position can become raising hands from late position. When you're in late position, the information you have about other players' hands is maximized and the information they have about your hand is minimized.

Sometimes, position refers to your seat location relative to other players. You're said to have position on a player when you act after that player. By forcing him to act first, you're giving him a chance to make the first mistake.

Most players realize that they can profitably play more hands from late position than from early position. But they often don't realize they should also be raising more often from late position than from early position. Don't just play more hands from late position—raise with them.

The reason you can profitably play more hands from late position than from early position, and play more aggressively, is that you have less to fear from a raise by another player—the more players left to act after you, the greater the chances of a raise. But late position also gives you a chance to observe displays of weakness from other players, allowing you to upgrade the value of your otherwise marginal hands. Raising with hands like A♥J♣ or A♥ 10♥ can become a solid value.

Just looking at your hand doesn't tell you how strong it is relative to the hands of other players. Many players come to poker looking for a system that tells them, "If I have these cards then I do this." Some hands are powerful no matter what, like a pair of Aces, but generally power doesn't just come from your cards. It comes from the whole situation. Judging a hand's relative strength and how it stacks up to the other players' hands requires you to compare your hand to the other hands. This is easier to do from late position—so that you don't have to act on your hand until they've already acted, giving you clues about the strength of their hands. The information that you can be gathering while the other players are acting is very valuable. Don't waste it, pay attention.

Using position to your advantage is an exercise in information management. The more people who have to act before you, the more information you have. This information is worth money to you if you use it properly.

Unlike seven-card stud, where playing position changes with the cards dealt, in games such as hold'em playing position is fixed (the same every betting round) and the risks of early position eventually become clear to even the most unobservant players. But simple observation alone can't be counted on to reveal the extra value of late position. Uncovering this value generally requires a little thought and analysis.

Aggression

Selective aggression is the single most important part of your game. There are many different reasons to bet:

- Betting the best hand to reduce the odds callers are getting to chase
- Betting strong draws to get odds on the call from weaker draws
- Betting draws so that better hands will fold
- Betting marginal hands so that draws will fold

Good things tend to happen when you bet, because a bet by you forces your opponents into a decision, and they have to react to your action. The more often you make them react to you, the more often they'll make a mistake. If you don't bet, they may make a mistake by betting when they should check or checking when they should bet. But if you do bet, they may make a mistake by calling when they should fold, folding when they should call (or should raise), or raising when they should call (or should fold).

You not only generate more ways for them to make a mistake by betting, but also the mistake on their part of folding when they should call is the most expensive mistake for them, and the best outcome for you. It's wildly profitable to you for them to consistently fold when they should call. Think about it. If everyone folded whenever you bet, then you'd eventually have all the money (in the form of winning the antes/blinds every time). But they won't fold if you won't bet. The cards aren't the key to winning at poker—betting is the key to winning.

Aggression is proactive. You're making them react to you. You put them in situations where they have to make tough choices, which gives them extra opportunities to make mistakes. Their mistakes are the source of profit in poker. Give them as many chances to make a mistake as you can. Raise.

Strong, unrelenting aggression often causes the other players to shift the focus of their thinking from the game itself to you specifically. Rather than thinking about their own hand and how they should play it, they'll think in terms of you, of what you're likely to do. At the extreme of this situation, you'll literally own the table in the sense that other players will begin to focus their attention on you rather than on their own hands.

Slowplay. One of the most overrated playing tactics in poker is slowplaying. Also called sandbagging, slowplaying is playing a strong hand passively in the initial rounds in the hope that your opponent will catch up to make a strong but second-best hand. The problem with this is that the very strong hands make most of their money when the opponent already has a strong second-best hand, or a strong draw to a second-best hand. Too many times in these situations he'll just slowplay right behind you.

I'm not saying you should never slowplay. Sometimes it's very appropriate. But many players tend to automatically slowplay whenever they have a big hand. And automatically slowplaying a big hand is a mistake. Really, automatically doing almost anything in poker is a mistake. But automatically slowplaying seems to be a frequent one.

Responding to Aggression. You aren't the only player at the table and you aren't the only player who'll be aggressive. Some of your opponents will be showing various degrees of aggression and you'll need to respond to them. How you respond when your opponents take the lead in the betting can be as important as your action when you take control.

The best response to aggression is player specific. Sometimes, you should preempt with aggression of your own. Sometimes, you should sandbag and let him make the first aggressive move. Sometimes, you should just respond passively and let him bluff his chips away. In deciding which response is best, you simply have to project how he'll react to various behaviors on your part. If a player likes to bluff too much, just check and let him bet.

Outs and Draws

It's important to get your money in the pot when your hand is best. But having the best hand doesn't always mean having the best in terms of poker rank. At any betting round when there are still more cards to come, you need to look at the odds you're getting from callers—not pot odds, but the number of active hands that will call a bet. Your hand is best when the odds that you will win the pot are greater than the odds you are getting from the number of callers. This doesn't mean your hand is the best poker hand right then—just that you have the best of it from a bet.

Sometimes, there can be a tradeoff between taking a bad position and getting good odds. This can happen when a couple of new players are posting extra blinds, so that the initial pot has dead money from, for example, four blinds rather than the usual two. This situation frequently occurs online because many players are coming and going, only playing for short times. Because of this extra dead money, it often pays to come in with a raise from out of position with hands like A♥ J♥ or even A♥ 10♥. This kind of situation is one of the subtle differences between online play and live games. The situation occurs in live games, but it occurs with much more frequency online.

Multiway Hands. An important strategic goal in split-pot games is to go after the whole pot, so don't get involved when you only have a draw for half the pot. This is why in seven-card stud hi/lo split you want to have an Ace, preferably suited with another low card, and in Omaha hi/lo split a suited Ace 2 is so powerful. These kinds of starting hands give you a start at the whole pot and give you more than one way to win a showdown. In all forms of poker, you want to look for hands that have more than one way of winning in a showdown, but it's particularly critical in hi/lo split games.

In seven-card stud, for example, if you start with a three flush you want it headed by an Ace for two reasons. One, if you make a flush you want it headed by an Ace—you don't want to end up with a second-best flush. Just as importantly, the Ace gives you a backup chance to win by pairing. This is why A♥ K♥ Q♥ is a much, much better start than A♥ 2♥ 3♥. They have the same flush and straight possibilities, but the A♥ K♥ Q♥ has many more ways to win by pairing a big card. Of course, in seven-card stud hi/lo split the relative value of these two hands is reversed.

Most players seem to recognize this more easily in hold'em, where the difference between K♥ Q♥ and 5♥ 6♥ is somehow more obvious to most. Always look for extra ways to win. If you don't have them, then you probably have a weak hand.

Midrange pocket pairs in hold'em also have this characteristic of giving you multiple ways to win a showdown. It's a common belief that pocket pairs like 6s, 7s, and 8s have to flop a set to win and that they should only be played against many opponents (to get good odds). Of course, fit or fold is a good strategy for these hands, but it's wrong to think the only flops that fit them are those that give sets. A pair of 8s is often an over pair to the flop and any of the middle pairs can hit the flop with a straight draw. Flopping a pair and a straight draw is a pretty good outcome in hold'em.

Chasing. A general principle of winning poker is to bet the best hand and let the losers call your bets while trying to catch up. "Don't chase" is a classic piece of poker wisdom.

This is usually good advice, but sometimes it's not. Sometimes, the pot is large enough to justify chasing. Sometimes, your draw is good enough to actually be ahead, even though it's not the best poker hand.

In hold'em and Omaha, the flop is a critical point in the game. One of the most frequent decisions is whether to chase or not and whether to take the lead with your draw if you do chase. This decision is made on the flop. In stud, you usually have to make this decision on fifth street, in seven-card stud hi/lo, you should usually make this decision earlier, on fourth street.

Chasing is about calling. The size of the pot and your position relative to the bettor and other active hands are key considerations when deciding whether to chase. If you're going to be chasing, you want to be chasing a large pot. You want to be getting the right odds. You also want to be the last to call the bet because you don't want your odds cut by having someone behind you raise.

Aggression with a draw is a behavior that many players find uncomfortable. But betting draws is a significant source of win in loose games. Betting a draw isn't about chasing and it's not a pot odds decision. It's a decision based on the winning chances of the hand, the odds you'll get from callers (not from the pot), and your image.

TELLS

Tells are part of the psychology of the game in that you need to understand the psychology of your opponents to correctly read their behavior. Reading tells from aggressive/tricky players is a different process from reading tells from passive/straightforward players.

The interpretation of tells is based on a determination of whether he is trying to deceive—he'll tend to be deceptive when he's aware you are watching and tend to act naturally when he's unaware or unconcerned whether you are watching. Tells aren't foolproof, but overall, paying attention to tells will win you an extra pot or two over time and save you a few bets in between.

Knowing which player is likely to bet or raise lets you time your aggression to achieve the goal you want for your bet. Knowledge is control. You can acquire knowledge from tells.

For example, if you are betting a draw, you want volume calls, and if you know the player on your immediate left will bet, you can check, then raise after players in the field have already called one bet. Knowing a player is weak often allows value bets that might otherwise be a little thin.

Tells aren't 100 percent reliable. When using tells, you do need to combine them with other information.

Reading Players

Reading players is the art of making a determination about your opponents' likely holdings. It is an art, but there is also some science to it.

Reading a player involves a study of the habits of that player, making a stereotypical categorization of the player, a knowledge of how certain types of players tend to behave, and an understanding of general principles of tells and acting.

Categorizing Opponents

The first step to reading a player is to categorize him.

At various points in the remainder of this book, you'll see me refer to your opponents with adjectives such as tight, passive, tricky, loose, aggressive, straightforward, weak, tenuous, rational, or irrational. These adjectives have some specific operational meanings that help categorize your opponents.

It's typical in poker books to categorize players along two independent dimensions: tight/loose and aggressive/passive. Tight players don't play many hands, loose players play a lot of hands. Aggressive players bet and raise a lot, passive players seldom bet or raise.

Generally, passive is considered bad, as is loose. Tight is considered good, as is aggressive. Of course, even the good traits of tight and aggressive can be carried to extremes. A player who plays way too tight is called a rock and a player who plays way too aggressive is called a maniac.

But there are problems with this traditional, two-dimensional view of poker players. One such problem was recently discussed on the Internet newsgroup rec.gambling.poker. The problem comes up in various situations, one being when interpreting the actions of a passive player. The traditional view is that bets by a passive player should be respected—the idea being that when a player who doesn't bet often wakes up and starts betting, he must have found himself with a good hand. But Abdul Jalib, the Internet nick of a Las Vegas poker pro who frequently contributes to these discussions, pointed out that this is just not true. You could easily be faced with a player who seldom bets but when he does bet he's almost always bluffing.

You can account for this possibility by considering a third dimension—along the lines of a straightforward/tricky dichotomy. Then it would be accurate to say you should respect the bets of a straightforward, passive player.

In my first book, I categorized opponents along four dimensions: tight/loose, aggressive/passive, tricky/straightforward, and weak/tenacious (I called it weak/tough in the previous book, but I like tenacious better). Since then, I've picked up a fifth dimension from some Internet discussions that I like: rational/irrational.

A tight player doesn't play many hands, a loose player plays a lot of hands. Notice that this dimension of player characteristics doesn't tell you much about how aggressive, tricky, or tough the player might be. Tight players are often weak, but not nearly often enough for it to make any sense to assume a tight player is weak.

An aggressive player bets and raises a lot with the hands he plays. (Note that an aggressive player can be tight or loose. The same with a passive player.) A passive player checks and calls with most of the hands he plays.

A tricky player tends to bluff or semibluff and slowplay a lot. He may intentionally give off fake tells. A straightforward player bets when he has a strong hand, and checks and calls when he has a draw or a weak hand. (Note that a tricky player is probably not a passive player.)

A weak player gives up easily and folds a lot. He always fears the worst, seeing monsters under the bed and running from them. A tenuous player hangs on, doesn't give up, and is hard to bluff successfully.

A rational player tends to make decisions based on ideas about his chances of winning money. He may be making mistakes and may have bad judgment about his money-winning potential, but winning money is his goal. An irrational player makes decisions based on emotional needs, rather than on financial considerations.

Most books that deal with categories of players do so along only two dimensions: tight/loose and aggressive/passive. In fact, one book, *The Psychology of Poker* (2000) by Alan Shoonmaker, is devoted entirely to this two-dimensional analysis of players. But, like a two-dimensional model of space, a two-dimensional model of poker players simply lacks depth. It's a superficial view with only superficial usefulness.

The Psychology of Poker isn't really about the psychology of poker. It presents a framework for categorizing players as aggressive/passive or tight/loose. It's a standard framework, one that almost all poker writers use. Shoonmaker borrows from the literature on management styles and takes the standard stereotypical poker player categories further than most. You might say he takes it too far. His focus on the individual opponent helps somewhat on how to react to a loose player as an isolated opponent, but doesn't help much in showing things such as how to adjust to having many loose callers acting before you (position).

I think the five dimensions I use to categorize players capture the important characteristics of player style and behavior. They don't have the mathematical nicety of being independent of each other, but you can't have everything. An example of where using four dimensions to categorize players differs from using just two is the question of when to bluff. You bluff weak players, who give up easily. This is simple enough. But when you think of players as having only two behavioral dimensions of tight/loose and aggressive/passive, it's not so simple. Some writers, such as Shoonmaker, suggest you should bluff tight, passive players, somehow assuming that tight, passive means weak. Although some tight, passive players are weak, not nearly enough of them are for you to be bluffing them indiscriminately unless you just want to bleed your chips off.

Don't fall into the trap of superficial player stereotypes. Pay attention to as many of the important playing characteristics of your opponents as you can. Player stereotypes are important. But they need to be complete, deep stereotypes, not superficial.

PATIENCE

None of the strategic concepts in this book will be of any use to you if you don't have patience. The long run can be a long time. And if you start out getting behind a little bit, it can take a very long time before you catch up. Patience is what separates a tight, aggressive, winning player from a maniacal, losing player.

The idea of the long run is often misunderstood; things don't even out in the long run, but they do average out. What is the difference?

If you start out a sequence of plays with a loss, you shouldn't expect an offsetting win in the future. The future has no memory. The long run doesn't mean offsetting wins and losses. It means that after time the effect of that initial loss on your overall average will be negligible.

Let's look at an example of tossing a coin.

My first five flips are all heads. So my initial count of heads and tails is:

Heads	Tails
5	0

Say the next 100 flips works out to be exactly fifty heads and fifty tails (the expected result). Then my count is:

Heads	Tails
55	50

I still have an excess of five heads. But what is happening is that the percent of times I flipped heads is converging to 50 percent:

Heads (%)	Tails (%)	
100	0	(after 5 flips)
52	48	(after 105 flips)

If I flip five heads then make 1,000 flips with half heads and half tails, the percentage of heads and tails gets even closer to 50 percent:

Heads (%)	Tails (%)	
100	0.0	(after 5 flips)
52.0	48.0	(after 105 flips)
50.2	49.8	(after 1,000 flips)

Nothing happens to offset the initial run of five heads. This is not what the law of large numbers says. The law of large numbers says that if you keep flipping, the run of five heads won't matter because it just doesn't count for much in the long run.

Poker is the same. If you have some bad luck, you won't have some good luck in the future to cancel it out. But if you play long enough, then some particular run of bad luck just won't count for much.

2

Hold'em

Hold'em is a game of big cards and position. The big pair rules in hold'em and the big pair from late position rules ruthlessly. One of the things that makes position so important in hold'em is that your position remains fixed from betting round to betting round. This gives you a strong strategic advantage when in late position. Daniel Negreanu, a poker tournament pro in Las Vegas and *Card Player* columnist, refers to the last four playing positions in hold'em as his "office." This is because late position is where he plays most of his hands, being much more hesitant to get involved from early position. This is the way to play hold'em. There's no need to get involved from early position, where it's hard to know whether you have the best of it or not because you have to act first. Betting with the best of it is what playing winning poker is all about. Wait a couple of hands, then you'll be the one acting last, you'll be the one with the information, you'll be the one who can bet or raise with some confidence.

GAME PROCEDURE

Hold'em has four betting rounds and is usually played with what's called structured betting: the first two betting rounds are at one limit and the last two are double that limit. For example, 10/20 or 3/6.

Hold'em games use a "button" to indicate a designated dealer for each hand. The button rotates in turn, but for the play of a hand the designated dealer is fixed. He doesn't actually deal, but the deal and the order of play are as if he were dealing. The first player to the left of the button posts a small blind bet of one-half the first round bet amount. For example, in 10/20 the small blind is $5. The next player (second to the left of the button) posts a large blind equal to the size of the first bet.

Before the Flop

The play starts with each player being dealt two cards face down. This is your private hand. Your hand will later be supplemented with five community cards. But for now you have two cards.

The first betting round starts to the left of the big blind, and he can either call the blind bet, raise, or fold. No checking in the first betting round. The betting rotates around to the small and big blind, and the big blind has an option to raise if no one has raised yet. All subsequent betting rounds begin with the first player to the left of the button. Only in the first round do the blinds act last.

The Flop

The second betting round commences after the flop has been dealt—three community cards placed face up in the middle of the table. These cards belong to everyone. If a pair comes on the flop, then everyone has at least a pair.

Before it's all over, there will be five cards in the center. Your final hand will be the best hand you can make from the combined seven cards of your private two-card hand and the five community cards on the board.

The flop betting begins with the first active player to the left of the button. This will either be one of the blinds or the first player to have acted preflop if both blinds folded preflop. The blinds are in kind of a special situation. On the first betting round, they are last to act, which is a very good position. But they'll be first in all subsequent betting rounds. So even though you already have at least some of your call money already in the pot, you should often play somewhat tight from the blinds. Calling too many raises from the blind because you already have part of the call in is a big leak for some players.

The Turn

The turn is a fourth community card, dealt face up on the board. Betting proceeds as on the flop, starting with the first active player to the left of the button. This isn't always the same player who was first on the flop, since, as a result of the flop action, the first player to act on the flop may have folded and be no longer active.

The River and Showdown

The river is the fifth and final face up community card. The betting proceeds as on the flop and turn. After the betting there is a showdown.

Reading the board and reading your hand might require a little practice. For example, don't get excited by two pair if one of the pairs is on the board. For example, say you have 7♦ 7♣ and the board is A♠ 5♦ 4♥ 4♣ 9♣. You have two pair, 7s and 4s. But any player with a single Ace, or even just a single 9 has a bigger two pair. And someone with a single 4 in their hand has three 4s and has you all beat. With a board of A♠ A♦ 8♥ 8♣ 9♣, you still have two pair, but now it's Aces and 8s, with a 9 kicker. Your 7s don't even play, no one at the table with an active hand has a worse hand than you.

If the board is A♣ Q♣ 7♣ 4♣ 2♣, then you're in that same situation, every player has a flush, and if you don't have a club in your hand, then no one has a lower flush than you. Anyone with any club in their hand has a bigger flush than you.

If you're confused by any of this, spend some time sitting at the kitchen table dealing out hands and boards.

HAND SELECTION: THE FIRST BETTING ROUND

In hold'em, if you're in early position (one of the first two or three players to act) for the first betting round, then you'll be in early position for every betting round. So it's important to only get involved with hands that don't require information on other players hands to judge the relative strength of your hand. Hands like A♦ A♥, J♥ J♦, and A♥ Q♦ are generally strong enough to withstand the risk of early position. Hands like 6♥ 7♥, A♥ 4♥, and 6♦ 6♥ aren't strong enough to overcome this risk.

If you play with the same players every day, you might want to sometimes open from early position with hands like 6♥ 7♥, A♥ 4♥, and 6♦ 6♥ for deceptive reasons. You don't want it to become too easy for them to put you on a hand. But generally, such hands aren't worth fooling with from early position.

From midposition or late position, it's important to distinguish between situations where no one has yet opened and those where someone has opened. And if someone has opened, it's important to distinguish whether he opened from early, mid-, or late position, and whether he opened with a raise. The reason the position of the opener is important is that the distribution of likely hands he holds depends partly on his position. Most players won't play as many hands from early position as they will from late position, and a player who opens in early position is more likely to have big cards, or even a big pair, than is one who opens from late position. This is true of even most of the worst players. There are players, for example, who won't play a pair of 6s from early position, but they will raise with it if they are the first ones in from a middle position. There are a few players who pay no attention to position at all, but they're rare.

Important Strategic Considerations in Hand Selection

Hold'em is more strategic and more action oriented than most other forms of poker. Small edges can take on large importance. This is primarily because of the community cards. Every player has five of seven cards in common. The difference between A♣ K♣ and A♣ J♣ might not seem like much, but it gets to be a pretty big difference when the flop is A♥ 7♦ 3♣ and you have an opponent with A♦ Q♦.

Hand Domination. Although the concept of hand domination exists in all forms of poker, it's a concept that has really only been formerly recognized in the hold'em literature. The concept isn't unique to hold'em, but its formalization is. A hand is said to be dominated if it has three or fewer outs. A pair of 5s is dominated by a pair of 6s because in order to improve to the best hand the pair of 5s must catch one of the two remaining 5s to win. An AJ is dominated by an AQ because the AJ must specifically catch one of the three remaining Jacks to improve to a better hand than the AQ. Of course, even then it has to hope the Queen doesn't also pair.

This is a very important concept in hold'em because of the community cards. If you hold an Ace, and pair your Ace, in a tight game you'll probably only get action on later streets if another player also pairs the Ace. You need to hope you're not the one with a dominated kicker.

Hands that are easily dominated, such as an Ace combined with a small card, or a very small pair, can be dangerous in hold'em, particularly from early position. The primary way to guard against the risk of domination is to be very careful in your initial hand selection. The difference between A♣ Q♦ and A♦ 8♣ or between A♣ 4♣ and Q♣ 4♣ is huge.

When No One Has Opened

If no one has opened, you can open with a raise with progressively weaker hands as fewer and fewer players are left to act after you. This is because of the equity involved in stealing the blinds (when you raise and no one calls). The fewer players left to act after you, the greater your chances of winning the blinds with a bet. If you're on the button, and everyone in front of you has folded, you can often raise with hands like A♦ 2♣, 9♣ 10♦, 5♣ 6♣, or even weaker. If the players on the blinds tend to fold to a raise too often, then you can open raise from the button with pretty much any two cards. Of course, you do need to be pretty sure they'll fold to be able to do this.

If no one has opened, there are three things you need to consider: your cards, your position, and the weakness of the players still left to act. Your position isn't measured by how many players have folded but by how many are left to act behind you. The more likely those players are to fold to a raise, the less you need to worry about them.

First to Act in Early Position. With many players left to act, you need to stick to hands that can stand a raise or a reraise: big pairs (from about 9s or 10s on up), big suited cards (like A♥ K♥ or K♥ J♥), and a few of the big card unsuited hands (like A♥ K♣, A♥ Q♣, or K♥ Q♣). If the game is a little tough, you might want to skip even some of these hands from early position. K♥ Q♣ or K♥ J♥ are hands that can sometimes turn out to not be nearly as strong as they might appear.

With the hands you'll be playing from early position, you'll usually want to open with a raise. The exception would be the very strongest hands (like A♥ A♦, maybe K♥ K♦) and the very weakest hands (like 9♥ 9♦, K♥ J♥, or K♣ Q♥). With the weaker hands, you should probably limp and call if anyone raises. With the stronger hands, you should often limp and reraise if anyone raises. Again, if you play against the same players all the time, you might want to mix this up a little bit. But don't overdo it. It is possible to be too tricky and deceptive.

Note that in short-handed games you are never in early position. For purposes of making playing decisions, early position means you have many players left to act, not that you are first to act.

First to Act in Midposition. If you have six of seven players behind you, and no one has yet acted, you're in a little better situation than you are in early position. The risk of a raise behind you has gone down and you can come in with a wider range of hands: midsized pairs like 7s or 8s become worth playing and you should consider hands like A♥ 9♥or 7♥ 6♥. From midposition, you should probably still play a little tight with offsuit hands, maybe adding hands like A♥ J♦ and Q♥ 10♦ to your arsenal.

First to Act in Late Position. In late position, your options really start to multiply. If you only have three or four opponents, with two of them the blinds who will have to act first on later betting rounds, then you're in pretty good shape.

You should probably come in with a raise on most hands that you play—and especially if the players on the blinds tend to play too tightly, you should probably play a lot of hands. Any suited Ace (A♥ 2♥, etc.) and most suited kings (K♥ 6♥ and better) become pretty good hands. More offsuit hands become playable. Again, depending on how tight the player left behind you, you might want to raise with hands as weak as 10♥ 9♣ or even 6♥ 7♣. You don't want to overdo this unless you are fairly sure there is a good chance a raise will win the blinds uncontested.

First to Act from the Button. Opening from the button depends almost entirely on how tight the two remaining opponents play their blinds. If you know nothing at all about how tight they are, or if they aren't very tight, then stick with the hands you'd play from mid- or late position. When opening from the button, you should almost always open with a raise. Even if the blinds aren't likely to fold, you have a huge positional advantage and you should capitalize on it.

But if they are tight and weak, so that they tend to give up their blinds easily, especially if the player on the big blind has this trait, then attack relentlessly, with any two cards in the extreme. Most opponents won't be so tight as to make it profitable to attack with any two cards, so you need to have something in reserve in case they call, but something like A♥ 7♣ or J♥ 6♥ is often more than you need from the button. Remember, you'll have position after the flop and that's a large advantage that can compensate for a weak start.

First to Act from the Small Blind. When everyone has folded except the blinds, and you are on the small blind, the situation is materially different than when you are on the button. This is because you'll have the disadvantage of being first to act on every betting round. This is a large disadvantage.

How you should proceed from the small blind depends on both how tight the big blind is and how aggressively he defends. You should tend to avoid getting involved with a highly aggressive player when you are out of position.

Some players like to chop when only the blinds are left. This means they just agree to not play if no one has voluntarily entered the pot, so each blind just takes his blind money back and doesn't play. If the other blind is willing to chop, than this is probably the best thing to do. The primary reason for chopping in low-limit games is that the pot will tend to remain small heads up and the rake will be difficult to overcome.

Against an Early or Midposition Opener

Opening from early position is a show of strength. Even if you limp in rather than opening with a raise, just being in early position shows that you aren't afraid of a raise, which is a show of strength. Just as you are selective in the hands you'll play from early position, so will most of your opponents. It's also important to make a distinction between when an early position opener comes in with a raise and when he limps. But whether he limps or raises, you need to always maintain an awareness that there's a good chance he has a very strong start.

When There Is an Early or Midposition Raiser. When there is an early position raise, you need to be careful with easily dominated hands—hands like A♦9♦, K♦10♦, J♦10♦, and even A♣ K♦. Against a very tight early raiser you should probably fold most of those easily dominated hands, certainly not reraise with them. An exception would be when there is an early raise followed by three or four cold callers. In this situation, you are getting good enough odds to overcome the risk of domination with hands like the above.

When There Is an Early or Midposition Limper. Beware of tricky players who limp from early position; they are often limping with big pairs or another big hand like A♦ K♦.

But when a straightforward player limps in early position, it's almost always because he either has a hand with weak high-card strength, like Q♦ J♦ (a loose, straightforward player might have Q♦ J♣ or even 9♦ 10♣) or a draw like 7♣ 6♣. In this case, you should be raising with many of those hands you'd consider folding against a tight early raiser.

Multiway Hands from Late Position. When you're in late position and four or five players have limped in ahead of you, you should usually raise with a wide range of both strong hands and drawing hands—hands like A♣ Q♦, A♣7♣, 7♣ 7♦, 9♣ 10♣, and so on.

When There Is a Late Position Opener

Opener Raised from Late Position. Players who open from late position often have weak hands. This tends to be particularly true of players who limp from late position. With only a few players left to act, it's very unusual for a late position opener to limp with a big hand. Most players will raise with a wide range of hands from late position, but the range of hands they'll limp with is restricted to weak hands. You should raise most late position limpers with a wide range of hands with both big card strength and drawing strength.

Opener Limped from Late Position. When a player comes in with a raise from late position, it's important to know something about that player's habits. Aggressive, tricky, or loose players might be raising with marginal hands in this situation.

PLAYING THE FLOP:
THE SECOND BETTING ROUND

Your hand selection at the initial betting round is an important decision. But it's usually not a difficult decision. Your play on the flop is often both a critical and difficult decision. You can be more precise about putting another player on a hand on the flop, but achieving this precision can be difficult.

Heads Up on the Flop

Heads up play doesn't always require that you have a strong hand; it doesn't even require that you have the best hand. It's enough that your opponent not have a good hand. At least it's enough if you play aggressively enough.

Aggression is your key weapon when playing heads up. Some players call this a pound, pound, pound strategy

How likely it is that naked aggression will work depends a lot on the texture of the flop. The more possible draws a flop shows, the less likely a bet will win it without a hand to back it up. A flop of 9♣ 8♣ 3♦ is much more likely to have hit an opponent than 9♥ 6♣ 2♦, and if your opponent is paying attention, he is more likely to think you're betting with a draw rather than a made hand if the texture shows a lot of possible draws. The importance of the texture of the flop extends to multiway situations also. In fact, it's probably more important in multiway situations. When the flop shows a lot of potential draws, overcards alone are seldom worth playing in multiway situations.

When You're First to Act. When you're heads up against weak opposition and you're first to act, you should just bet—typical players will fold when the flop misses them, and it will miss them often enough to make a bet worthwhile.

If you bet into an aggressive player when heads up on the flop, he'll often just make an automatic raise, just to see how you'll react.

Against highly aggressive opponents, you should often check, call with as little as Ace high.

When You're Last to Act. Unless you're up against a very tricky player, you should almost always bet if you're heads up and he checks to you. If he bets, you need to consider how aggressive he is and the texture of the flop in terms of how likely it is he's betting a draw. If he's an aggressive player, he'll bet a lot of hands and you should often raise with what you might think of as marginal hands in other circumstances.

Multiway Hands on the Flop

But most of the time you won't be heads up. You need to make a judgment about your hand and how it stacks up to all the other hands that are still active. When this involves four, five, or six players, this judgment can be problematic.

If there are three or four (or more) active hands seeing the flop, it's important to bet your good hands like top pair with a good kicker. Try to drop as many players as you can. In accomplishing this, your position relative to the button isn't as important as your position relative to a likely bettor or raiser. For example, if you are in early position in a raised pot and a very aggressive player is on the button, then it might be a good idea to check your strong hands, expecting him to bet so that you can raise, facing those players after you with two bets cold, and putting pressure on them to fold. The more active hands there are on the flop, the more important this is. With few opponents, it's often right to slowplay on the flop, waiting until the turn when the bet size doubles before you raise. Waiting is seldom a good idea against a large field. There's just too many bad things that can happen on later streets if you let a lot of opponents in cheaply on the flop.

Position Relative to the Probable Aggressor. On the flop, you should often think of your position relative to the aggressor rather than relative to the button. For example, if you're first to act but you know the opponent on your immediate left will bet if you check, then you effectively have last position. You can be fairly sure of when a particular opponent will bet surprisingly often.

Preflop raisers often automatically bet the flop. Some players will automatically bet from late position on the flop if it's checked to them.

Many players telegraph their intent to bet by prematurely reaching for their chips. When they are reaching for their chips in a natural way, as opposed to putting on a show of reaching for chips, they usually intend to bet. I'll get into that a little more in chapter 9 (tells and hand reading).

Draws in Multiway Hands. By multiway, I mean more than two active hands. Most hands end up being played multiway. Games that don't have most hands competed for multiway are usually tight games that aren't going to last long.

Strong draws should usually be played aggressively in multiway hands.

By draw, I mean a flush draw or a straight draw with overcards. Flush draws are almost always strong draws. Straight draws not always. If you have two to a straight or flush in your hand and two on board, then assuming your straight cards have no gaps, you have eight cards you can catch to make your straight, or nine cards you can catch to make your flush.

It looks like there isn't much difference between a flopped straight draw and a flopped flush draw, right? Wrong. There is a world of difference between the two draws. Flush draws are almost always stronger, for three reasons:

1. There are nine ways to complete a flush draw, versus eight ways for a straight draw
2. A flush beats a straight
3. The card that makes you a straight might give someone else a flush or flush draw

ON THE TURN

You should usually be aggressive on the turn. If you think you have a strong hand and a scare card falls on the turn (like a card that might make someone a flush, or might make someone a bigger pair than yours), you should usually bet. Sometimes you should bet and fold to a raise, sometimes you should bet and call a raise. Whether you bet, and what you should do if you bet and get raised, is usually more dependent on the players involved and their habits and general tendencies than on the cards themselves. For example, if you have top pair and a flush card falls on the turn, then you should probably bet and fold to a raise only against a passive, straightforward opponent. Against more aggressive or tricky players you might still find it best to bet but you shouldn't fold to a raise.

When He Might Be Semi-Bluffing

Many players will wait until the betsize doubles on the river to raise with a strong hand. Also, many players will semibluff if they pick up a flush draw on the turn.

A semibluff is what used to be called raising with outs. David Sklansky introduced the term semi-bluff in his book *The Theory of Poker*. It's a certain kind of raise that's made before the last round of betting, when there are more cards to come, and there is some chance that the raise will win the pot right there. It's a semi-bluff rather than just a bluff if you also have some fallback, some chance you'll end up winning the showdown anyway. Raising with a flush draw is an example of a semi-bluff. Basically, the idea is that you might win the pot right now, but if you don't, all is not lost because you might still improve to the best hand.

If the board looks like there is a chance your opponent has a draw (such as having two hearts on the board) then you need to always consider the possibility that your opponent is semi-bluffing when he raises before the last betting round.

THE RIVER—THE FINAL BETTING ROUND

Should you bet on the river? You should when you figure to win if you get called. But, not always. You should certainly bet if you're last to act and think that it's more likely than not that you'll win if he calls. But, what if you're first and your opponent tends to bluff a lot. Then maybe you shouldn't bet, maybe you should check and let him bluff.

You should not simply bet because you think you have the best hand. The question is whether you figure to have the best hand if you're called.

Should you bluff on the river? Are you first? Do you have reason to think he was on a draw and missed? Is he the kind of player that will tend to call with any Ace, no pair hand? Are you last? Is he the kind of player who tends to check most hands on the river? Or does he only check when he can't beat top pair? You need to know something about the player in general and the specifics about the way this hand developed when deciding whether or not to bluff on the river.

Should you call on the river? If he bets, should you call? Sometimes, even if you're sure you have the bettor beat, you shouldn't call. This would be in multiway pots where there are players behind you who you are just as sure they have you beat. Calling on the river in a multiway pot often takes a stronger hand than calling when heads up. This is true even when multiway action has made the pot much bigger than what a typical heads up pot size would be.

When should you overcall? An overcall is a special case of calling. It means you are the second player to call, after a third player has bet. When another player bets and a second player calls, you need a much stronger hand to call than if it was just a single player betting. A player who calls on the river isn't bluffing. He can beat a bluff. If you have a hand that can only beat a bluff, then you almost always fold if one player bets and another calls.

I recently played a hand where I was third to act. The other two players had been checking and I'd been betting. The top card on the flop was a 9, I had a 9 with a King kicker. On the river, an Ace fell that also put three hearts on the board and the first player bet right out. He was a straightforward player who'd been at the table for a few hours and he hadn't been bluffing. I wasn't sure whether to call or not. I was pretty sure I was beat, but there was probably some slim chance he was bluffing. I was leaning toward folding and probably would have folded anyway, but when the second player called his bet, my fold was cinched. She didn't call with nothing. It was very likely that the first player had me beat, and almost a certainty that one of the two had me beat. I folded quickly. He had a flush, and she had the same hand as me, a 9 with a King kicker. This is an example of needing a stronger hand to overcall than to call and also an example of the value of last position.

GENERAL COMMENTS ON THE GAME

Because your final hand is formed as the best five cards out of the seven available, some people describe hold'em as a variation of seven-card stud. But strategically, the two games are very different. Hold'em is more likely a derivative of spit-in-the-ocean, a community card game popular in some home games. The community card feature makes hold'em a very different game from seven-card stud. In seven-card stud, if you catch a second pair, your hand has improved. In hold'em, if you catch a second pair, by having the board pair, it's not clear at all that your hand has improved.

Counterfeiting

Getting counterfeited simply means catching a card on the board that is redundant or renders another card in your hand unusable or unnecessary. A redundant card is a card that is useless because there exists another card that serves the same function.

A simple example from hold'em is K♣ K♦ K♥ K♦ A♠ on the board in hold'em—any Ace in your hand is redundant. If you have an Ace in your hand, the Ace on the river would counterfeit you.

Counterfeiting frequently occurs with straights. If you have Q♥ T♥ and the board is J♠ 9♥ 8♦ 4♣, a Ten on the river counterfeits your hand by being a redundant card for a straight. If also means you no longer have the nuts.

A small two pair is sometimes easily counterfeited. For example, A♠ A♥ 3♥ K♦ K♣ counterfeits you when you have 5♦ 5♠. The last King pretty much destroys your hand. Likewise, a King on the river counterfeits your two pair when you have 9♠ 8♠ and the board is K♦ 9♣ 8♣ 5♦.

Even full houses can get counterfeited. If you have T♣ T♦ and the board is K♠ K♥ T♥ 5♦, a King on the river makes one of the Tens in your hand redundant, and would help someone holding T♠ 2♣ catch up to you.

BOOKS ON HOLD'EM

The last twenty years has seen a lot of poker books on the market, many of them have been on hold'em. Some are pretty good books, and some not so good, but, I think even the bad books have something to offer. Hold'em is a complex game and every author has added a little bit of unique insight into various aspects of the game.

One of the better hold'em books is a book I wrote, *The Complete Book of Hold'em Poker* (Lyle Stuart 2001). Most poker book authors tend to look at the game from a fixed perspective, often a different perspective from other writers, but a perspective that seldom changes within their own work. Authors tend to make fixed assumptions about what typical behavior from your opponents is. My book is no exception. Although I tried to look at the game from a variety of perspectives, most of the book focuses on loose games, the value of getting the right odds on your draws and playing them aggressively and on similar topics that are often of critical importance in low-limit games. I do this because I think it's a neglected perspective among the hold'em books.

The first worthwhile book written on hold'em was *Hold'em Poker* (1997) by David Sklansky. Originally published in 1978, this is a classic that every hold'em player should read, if only for its historical value. But it has some drawbacks. It was written when the standard game had a single blind half the size of the small bet. This was a structure that tended to have small pots, and draws were unimportant in this game. Also, it's a little pricey, so you might try an interlibrary loan at your local public library.

The book was updated in 1997 to reflect the change in blind structure that has occurred in most cardroom hold'em games. However, the update is generally superficial: many places just have footnotes that say that some of the advice is really no longer true. But even with all its shortcomings, it's still a good book. Many of the general principles discussed in the book apply to any structured-limit game. For example, Sklansky offers a good discussion on semi-bluffing. There is also an interesting section on the kind of flops you're most likely to see with various hands.

He was heavily influenced by the games in Las Vegas at the time and those games tended to be fairly tight by today's standards and compared with typical games outside of Las Vegas. If you find yourself in a tight/passive or loose/passive game, then much of what Sklansky offers in this book will be useful to you. Also, some cardrooms have spread-limit games where the initial blinds are very small and subsequent bets can be made within a range of allowable bets. These games tend to start with the same kind of small pots that the games Sklansky writes about had. So, if you're playing in a 1-4-8-8 spread-limit game, you might find Sklansky's hold'em book worthwhile.

Winner's Guide to Texas Hold'em Poker (1996), by Ken Warren, focuses specifically on those 1-4-8-8 spread-limit games. It's the only book on the market that I'm aware of that has an intentional focus on spread-limit games where the initial blind money is very small, compared to the size of future bets. The relatively low-limit games Warren addresses are often populated by many bad players and a common strategy for these games is to just sit and wait for the money to flow to you.

Lou Krieger has two books on basic hold'em: *Hold'em Excellence: From Beginner to Winner* (1999) and *More Hold'em Excellence:*

A Winner for Life (1999). A major plus for both these books is that Krieger is both a writer and a poker player, as a consequence, they are well written. This is not the normal situation in most poker books.

Although the two books don't really overlap much, they are very similar. In both books, Krieger takes a heavy approach in favor of patience and discipline. Concerns about hand domination seem very prevalent in the first book. *Hold'em Excellence* is aimed more directly at the beginning player and most of the advice is intended at keeping you out of trouble situations. It's a good approach for beginners and is a valuable book to read.

More Hold'em Excellence is meant for slightly more experienced players and provides more discussion on how to exploit the mistakes of others rather than how to avoid mistakes yourself.

Neither of the Kreiger books really offer much that can't just as well be found elsewhere, they don't really have anything unique to offer. But, both are readable and worth reading if you haven't already read a lot of poker books.

Like the Warren book, *Winning Low Limit Hold'em* (2nd edition, 2000) by Lee Jones is aimed at playing in low-limit games in public cardrooms, but this book is about low-limit with structured betting, rather than spread limits. The difference is that the structured games have more blind money in the pot to start and it's important to play more aggressively from the beginning where more passive play in early betting rounds is sometimes more appropriate in spread limit games with small blinds. It's a good book but I think he missed the point when it comes to playing in very loose games.

Even if you don't play in the low-limit games Jones addresses, this is a good book to read if you often find yourself in loose-passive games. He's heavily influenced by authors like David Sklansky and Mason Malmuth, but Jones writes much better than they do and his book is better edited and organized.

Hold'em for Advanced Players (1999) by David Sklansky and Mason Malmuth, was originally published in 1988. A second edition, with some new material, has recently been published. The book has a strong orientation towards ideas of hand domination and fancy plays, playing in a way to misrepresent your hand. It's geared mostly towards attacking loose-passive players with a strong focus on plays like semi-bluffs. It provides good coverage of many profitable deceptive plays that work well against small fields of weak players and covers a lot of material that gives you strong clues in reading tougher players that you're likely to find at tight or typical mid-limit tables. If for no other reason than it's a widely read book, you might want to read this book. I used to consider it a must read, but I no longer think this. The literature on hold'em has grown a lot, and this book really doesn't offer anything unique. It's overpriced, poorly written and organized, and your book dollars can almost certainly find a better place to be spent.

The new material that's been added to this new edition is mostly on short-handed play and playing in loose, wild games. The heads up material in the short-handed play section is good and well worth reading. The material for play in loose, wild games suffers from the author's tendency to stress ideas that stem from a fear of domination and an affinity for deception—two strategic perspectives that don't really add much value to play in very loose/very aggressive games.

Championship Hold'em (2000), by Tom McEvoy and T.J. Cloutier, tries to be a lot. It presents itself as a book aimed at all hold'em players, novices and professionals alike. This is a pretty big target. When writing a book, the big targets are much harder to hit than the small ones. It has a strong focus on avoiding hand domination and heads up conflicts between made hands and draws. A wide range of players will find the book interesting. It's not a book for a rank beginner, however.

The structure of the book is unusual. It has some chapters written by McEvoy, some by Cloutier, and most of the book consists of transcripts of conversations between McEvoy and Cloutier. This is not a typical book format, but it works well for this book.

The first chapter, by Cloutier, sets the tone with a list of eighteen "Key Concepts for Winning at Limit Hold'em." The traditional list of this sort might contain items like hand selection or check-raising. Not Cloutier's list. He lists items like watch your opponents and remember that kickers are important. He doesn't give you a set of rigid rules—he just gives you guidelines for thinking. Although the book as a whole does go into technical details about hand selection, when to raise, and other topics, this first chapter sets the tone of the general approach—this book is about thinking during the game.

My main criticism of the book is that it overemphasizes the idea of avoiding trouble. But if you're going to make mistakes, this is a mistake that is often not a mistake.

Mid-limit Hold'Em Poker (2002), by Bob Ciaffone and Jim Brier, is aimed directly at experienced hold'em players. There's no introductory material and the book dives right into hand example after hand example. The book will probably go right over the head of most readers, but once you've spent some time at the tables, this is a book you'll want to read and think about.

Another good book is *Inside the Poker Mind: Essays on Hold'Em and General Poker Concepts* (2000) by John Feeney. This book is a little more accessible to the beginning player, but it does tend to address games that are a little tougher than the typical low-limit game you'll find in most casinos. But it's well written and will give you lots to think about.

3

Seven-Card Stud

Seven-card stud is a game of patience and live cards. A popular book on seven-card stud in the 1970s was subtitled *The Waiting Game*. This is an apt subtitle. All poker games are games of patience, but it's especially so in the low-limit, no-ante, high-rake seven-card stud games typically found in cardrooms. Tight is right in these games.

The no-ante, low bring-in structure means the pots start out very small, so there isn't much money to chase. These games are also an exception to the general rule that aggression is good. This is not to say that you should be ultra passive in these games. If you're going to err, it's still right to err on the side of aggression. Aggression is worthwhile when the pots are worth taking risks to increase your chances of winning the pot. But pots in the no-ante seven-card stud games tend to start out small, and often remain small. On the early streets, when the pot is small, aggression is usually misplaced. If you have the best hand, you'll just end up with a small pot; if you don't have the best hand, you're just making a big pot for the player who does.

Stick with situations where you're pretty sure you're starting with the best hand. But don't overplay your hands even when you do think they are best.

GAME PROCEDURE

The game starts with each player being dealt two cards face down and one card face up. The player with the lowest ranking up card has a forced bet—called a bring-in. This player must bet a specified amount, typically an amount significantly less than the bet limit. The game is usually played with a $1 to $5 spread limit and the bring-in bet must be at least $1. This bring-in provides an initial pot, taking the place of an ante. The bring-in must bet, he cannot check. Subsequent players then act in turn to either call the bring-in, raise, or fold.

Then four cards are dealt to each player face up, with a betting round after each card. At each round, the betting starts with the player with the high hand showing.

The final card is dealt face down, followed by the final betting round and a showdown. The most common betting structure you'll find in cardrooms is a $1 to $5 spread limit. This game typically has no ante, a $1 bring-in, and bets or raises can be anything between $1 and $5 (with the proviso that any raise must at least equal the previous bet).

The game is also sometimes played with a higher spread limit, sometimes $2 to $10 or even $5 to $25. These higher spreads are often played with an ante. In some cardrooms, primarily in the northeastern United States and on the Internet, you'll also find structured betting. These games have an ante and fixed betting limits. Typically, the first two rounds are at one limit and the last three rounds are at twice that limit. The seven-card stud discussed here focuses on the no-ante, spread-limit, low-limit variety most often found. In a game with antes, you should tend to attack more aggressively in the early betting rounds to win the antes. Also, in a game with antes the pot is more often large enough to make it worth chasing on the early streets. I'm going to focus on the typical no-ante game structure.

THIRD STREET: HAND SELECTION AND THE FIRST BETTING ROUND

Of course, the best starting hand is three of a kind, but this won't happen often. More often, you'll be deciding whether to play hands like (6♥ 6♠)K♥ or (J♥ 10♥)Q♦.

How you play most hands, and even whether you play them at all, depends on your position relative to the opener and the exposed upcards of the other players. Paying attention to exposed cards can be critical in this game. It can be very important to know whether the cards you need for your draw are live or not; the only way to know this is to pay attention to cards that are being folded.

Three of a Kind

How you should play three of a kind depends on how big your trips are and your position. The size of your trips matter not so much because of the difference in strength between a (2♥ 2♣) 2♦ and a (A♥ A♣) A♦ but because of the different effect on your opponents when you raise with an exposed Ace versus an exposed deuce. When you make a raise on third street in seven-card stud, your opponents will, of course, assume you have some kind of hand strength. But they'll tend to make a judgment about what kind of strength primarily by considering your upcards.

Early Position Trips. When you are in early position, the pot will be very small—in the $1 to $5 spread-limit games, the bring-in is usually just $1. You have a very strong hand and will probably win the pot. So you want to get that pot as large as you can. The way to do this from early position is to limp, enticing others to call. A raise, with the small pot, will discourage callers, which is not what you want to do at all.

When you limp with trips, you're hoping someone else will raise so you can backraise. With a large card showing, your opponents won't automatically assume you have trips if you backraise. They won't even assume you have a pair. But such an aggressive move

with a small card showing will suggest the possibility of trips to ob-
servant opponents and they'll certainly put you on at least a small
pair with a big kicker. So, with small trips you might want to forego
the backraise if someone raises. Deception is always important, but
in stud, deception involving your door card can be especially useful.

Late Position Trips. If you're one of the last to act on the first betting round, you should usually raise with big trips (Aces, Kings, and
Queens) but just call with small trips. The reason for this is that a
raise with a big card showing will seem natural—they'll tend to
think you either have a big pair, or a hidden pair with a large kicker.
With big trips, the best way to disguise your hand is often to just
play it straightforwardly. But with a small card showing, a show of
strength can raise suspicion among your opponents if you get very
aggressive too early.

Big Pairs

By big pair, I mean Aces, Kings, and sometimes Queens. Queens
would be considered a big pair if there are no Kings or Aces showing among your opponents' upcards. Big pairs should be played
similarly to trips, but seldom should be slowplayed. The exception
might be Aces from out of position. An opponent with a small pair
doesn't have that far to go to catch up with you and you shouldn't
give him a free ride. It matters whether your pair is exposed or
hidden. (An exposed pair has one face up and one face down. A hidden pair has both cards face down with a face up kicker.)

Hidden Pairs vs. Exposed Pairs. A hidden pair is slightly
stronger than an exposed pair because with a hidden pair your
hand is not exposed when you make trips—if you have (A♦ 4♥)
A♣ and catch A♥ on a later street, everyone can see you have at
least a pair of Aces and they'll tend to not play very aggressively.
You'll win more bets if you make trips with a hidden pair. The
strength of a hand isn't just about how many pots it will win. It's

also about how much money it will win. Poker is about the money, not about winning pots.

But a big pair is strong enough either way and you should play it as such, especially playing the exposed big pair aggressively in the early rounds, when the situation is right. It's much easier to be sure of a big pair in early betting rounds than it is to be sure of it in later rounds when it hasn't improved.

Live Cards. It's important that your cards be live. This means it's important that you don't see any cards of the rank of your pair or kicker among the exposed cards of your opponents' (or of your suit if you have a flush draw). So it's important to keep track of the cards that have been folded. This is much easier said than done.

Ashley Adams, the author of *Winning 7-Card Stud* (2003), suggests this task can be simplified by remembering cards that have been folded. There is no need to remember upcards that are still visible. You might miss a few this way at first, but with some practice it should start working more smoothly for you. Try to remember the cards in numerical or rank sequence, not in the sequence they've been folded. For suits, you need to pay attention to any of your suit that have been folded or to any suit that has had a lot of cards folded. Adams says this is the procedure he follows, and it seems to work well for him.

Medium Pairs

With medium-ranked cards, like Jacks, 10s, 9s, and maybe even Queens or 8s, the difference between value of hidden pairs versus exposed pairs increases. Also, it becomes more important that your cards be live, that your kicker be live, and that you have a two flush to go with your pair. (9♥ 9♣) 8♥ is much stronger than (9♥ 8♦) 9♣. Of course, (9♥ 9♣) 8♥ loses that extra edge if it doesn't improve on fourth street.

Your position and the presence of overcards to your pair (and to your kicker) among your opponents' upcards starts to take on significance with midsized pairs.

Here's an example of a situation where a medium-sized pair should probably be folded. I am dealt a (5♠ 10♣) down and a 10♠ up. The low card (bring-in) is a 3♦ and the various upcards include an 8, a 5, a King, a 9, a Queen, and another 10. The King, 9, and Queen are all behind me. After the 3 brings it in, the 8 and the 5 fold. Should I play this pair?

No, I shouldn't. I've got one 5 gone, and one 10 gone. My two-card flush is alive but this is a long shot, because my pair isn't live and my kicker is small and not completely alive. And I have two players behind me with bigger upcards than my cards. A pair of 10s isn't a bad starting hand, but this situation is a pretty easy fold in a no-ante $1 to $5 game.

If you're playing in a higher limit game, with antes, and if there's some chance that a raise will steal the antes, then a raise might be appropriate, but even then it's close. In the typical $1 to $5 game with no antes, the risk that a player behind you has your pair beat isn't large, but it's too large to be worth the gamble. Because of all your dead cards, your chances of catching up are pretty slim.

Kickers. Your kicker starts to matter a lot when you have a medium pair. For a hand to be playable, you need all three starting cards working together. If you have a pair of Aces, then any kicker works with it for Aces up potential. But with a smaller pair, you need a good-sized kicker to have a draw at a high two pair. Medium-sized two pair, like 9s and 6s for example, are not strong hands in seven-card stud and are probably overall money losers for most players. Actually, medium-sized two pair are probably long-term money losers for most players in any popular form of poker today. A lot of players seem to think all two pair are alike, and this is far from correct.

Your kicker can also be working if it gives you a two flush or two straight—(9♥ 9♣) 3♥ can be playable in more situations than (9♥ 9♣) 3♦. These small edges matter, and they tend to matter even more in marginal situations.

Small Pairs

Small pairs should usually be folded, but depending on position, action, kickers, and live cards, they might be playable.

It's always important to have live cards in stud, but it's of critical importance when you have a mediocre start such as a small or moderate-sized pair that is very unlikely to win without improvement.

For example, let's say you're dealt (8♣ 8♠) Q♠. Normally, this is a decent start. It's not a big pair, but it's totally hidden and your kicker is somewhat large. I was recently dealt this hand and the situation was even better in that I had perfect position on third street, the bring-in (a 3) was on my left, meaning I was last to act on third street.

But one of the exposed cards was an 8, hurting my drawing strength quite a bit. The 8 folded, but a King and an Ace called the bring-in. It was a loose game and two smaller cards also called. Then a Jack raised. That raise pretty much cinched it. That pair of 8s wasn't worth playing.

The Jack was raising while looking at three overcards to his Jack. There was a real good chance he had me beat. Making trip 8s was unlikely with the 8 gone. And even if I made Queens up, it was likely that I would be beat by either Kings up or Aces up. There was just too much competition and I had too little of a chance, even though I was getting good money odds on a call.

But in a different situation a small pair can be a strong hand. Another recent hand involved me starting with a pair of 7s. This one I played, even though some of the characteristics of the hand weren't as strong. The hand itself wasn't as strong, but the situation was more advantageous, making the relative strength better.

I was dealt (7♦ 3♠) 7♥. Note that not only is a pair of 7s smaller than a pair of 8s, this time I had a split pair, a very small kicker, and no two-card flush draw. This wasn't really very strong.

But the upcards I was looking at were three 2s, a 4, an 8, and two Aces. My cards were completely live, and most of the other players' cards weren't. Only one player had a higher live upcard than me. Looking at two opponents with an Ace up is a much better situation than looking at only one opponent with an Ace. When that 8 folded to the bring-in, I had an easy raise. Even if all I won was the $1 bring-in, a raise in this situation didn't carry much risk with it. It was unlikely anyone had a better hand, and if they did, it was okay because my cards were live.

Medium-sized pairs are not strong hands, but they can become worthwhile in the right situation. Very small pairs, such as 2s, 3s, or 4s, are seldom worth bothering with under any circumstance. You might sometimes make an exception with them if your third card is an Ace, your hand is completely alive, and there isn't much risk of a raise.

In an article in *Card Player* magazine, Mike Caro makes the argument that a very small pair with an Ace is sometimes an exception to the general rule that it's better to have a hidden pair than a split pair. The reason is that catching a 2 with a holding of (2A)2 usually won't scare your opponents away while catching an Ace to (22)A will almost always scare them away. It's a weak argument though. Aces up is much more vulnerable than three 2s because the trips have a much greater chance of improvement. So having them tend to fold if you catch Aces up isn't really all that bad an outcome. But it is an interesting viewpoint to think about.

Flush Draws

Not all flush draws are created equal. A flush draw without anything extra going for it should probably be folded. But many flush draws do have something extra. If it has that little something extra, it might be worth taking off a card and seeing if it improves on fourth street.

Sometimes, just a couple of big cards is enough extra to turn a folding hand into a raising hand. For example, a hand like (2♠ K♠) Q♠ can be a strong start. Of course, it needs to have the spades and the Kings and Queens be live to have significant strength. And probably not be against an exposed Ace.

I recently had this hand when the other players' upcards included two Kings. There were no Queens, no Aces, and no spades showing though. Here, my King was dead, but my door card was very alive. Catching a Queen after raising on third street would probably have been enough to win the pot. That, combined with the spades being completely alive, made it worth a raise after another player had called the bring-in.

But it's probably only slightly best to raise. You might want to just call the bring-in from middle position with this drawing hand, hoping to entice more callers. I think it's close.

Three to a Royal. Three cards to a royal flush give you a lot of ways to win. There are nine cards you can catch to give you a big pair plus the flush and straight possibilities. If no players' upcards are overcards to your cards, and your cards are live, then you have a very strong hand. Play it accordingly.

Ace High Flush Draw. An Ace high flush draw also gives you a few ways to win. The Ace is key for two reasons: you can win by pairing the Ace and if you make a flush, you'll have an Ace high flush and be less likely to be beaten by some other player's bigger flush. The consideration of having a big flush is an important one in stud. If you make a flush, the distribution of the other cards is such that the likelihood of someone else also making a flush in a different suit increases. If there are two flushes out, you want the best, not the second best. This is a recurring theme in initial hand selection in all forms of poker—don't even get involved when it's likely that the best you can hope for is second best.

Other Flush Draws. Flush draws other than three to a royal, or an Ace high flush draw are usually not worth playing unless you're in late position on third street and can see the next card cheaply. There are exceptions, such as the one I gave earlier, but the exceptions involve special circumstances. You can also often play three midsized cards to a straight flush for one more card, but only if you're in late position, no one has raised, and both your flush and straight cards are live.

Other flush draws should usually not be played in no-ante, $1 to $5 seven-card stud.

Straight Draws

Unless the hand falls into one of the previous categories, three cards to a straight aren't worth playing. Straights aren't that easy to make and they aren't that strong when you make them.

Tactical Considerations on Third Street

When Should You Raise? It's often important to thin the field in stud games. Pairs tend to lose a lot of value when there are many players competing against you. In hold'em, you'll often want to be raising from late position with hands that you wouldn't even play from early position. Part of the reason for this is the power of fixed position at every betting round in hold'em. This is not the case in stud. Also, you will not always be more likely to raise from late betting position. You probably won't have that late position in later betting rounds of stud.

There are no standard rules of thumb for raising in stud. Such rules would require too much simplification to be very useful, because stud is a very situation-oriented game. It's a tactical game and the tactical situation is always changing. Among other things, the deceptive value of a raise isn't always the same.

Of course, it's very important to have live cards, but live cards aren't always enough to warrant an early raise.

For example, if you have a hidden big pair, you have a strong hand, but if you have a very small door card, a raise might scare away all your customers, leaving you winning just the bring-in. The reason the raise with a small door card tends to scare them is that they assume you must have something, and since what they see isn't much, they tend to imagine the worst. You do want to thin the field, but with a no-ante game you also want some players—you want to get some money in the pot besides the bring-in. But a raise with that small door card gives your hand away; the other players won't suspect you're raising with a pair of 4s, they'll suspect a hidden big pair.

In this sense, a big hidden pair with a midsized kicker showing is a lot stronger than the same hand with a very small kicker showing. Not because the kicker is more powerful, but because the midsized kicker is more deceptive.

How Much Should You Raise? The bring-in bet in the typical $1 to $5 game is $1. You can raise as much as $5, making it $6. You should often not raise at all from early position with a very strong hand. If there are no antes, a raise will often result in winning the dollar. With weaker hands, like a pair of Queens with one of your Queens showing in another hand, you might want to go ahead and raise, since winning the dollar might be as good as you're going to get. But it also might be just as well to go ahead and fold a hand like that from early position. Not that it's not a good start. It's just that when there's no money in the pot, most hands just aren't worth fooling with. If it's very likely everyone will fold to a raise, go ahead and raise and take the dollar. If not, then just fold it.

With a big hand that has some deception value, like an (AA)9 hand, you can go ahead and raise from early position because they'll put you on a pair of 9s and they won't fear that much. But don't raise the full amount—just raise a dollar or two. With the same hand from late position, after a couple of limpers have put some money in the pot, you can raise the full amount, or at least $3 or $4.

How much you should raise depends on how strong you really are and your position. With a really strong hand, you should make a small raise from early position and a large raise from late position. With a vulnerable hand, you should probably tend to make a large raise from early position and maybe not raise at all from late position.

Whether a situational hand is strong or vulnerable depends on more than the hand itself. For example, (KK)9 is generally a pretty good starting hand. But if an Ace is showing in an opponent's up-cards and you're already in early position, thus having to act before the Ace does, you're much more vulnerable than you would be if you were in later position and could act after the Ace had folded. Also, the more Kings and 9s showing in other players' upcards, the more vulnerable the (KK)9 is because of its reduced chances of improvement. The more vulnerable the hand is, the more impor-tant it is to either raise or fold rather than call. If you play a vulner-able hand, you want to do so aggressively in an attempt to win the pot as quickly as possible. The stronger the hand is, the more you can slowplay it in hopes of winning a larger pot.

Fixed rules of thumb just won't do the trick in deciding what to do. As such, you need to take in all the factors you can and make a judgment based on the totality of the situation. This doesn't always lead to an obvious course of action. The main point is that you should tend to give up when the pot is small, but when the pot starts to get a little larger you should be a little more aggressive in trying to win it.

FOURTH STREET: THE SECOND BETTING ROUND

If you started with a draw, and the pot wasn't raised on third street, you should usually fold to a bet if you don't improve on fourth street. If the pot had been raised on third street, it might be worth seeing one more card, even if you don't improve, but only if you can see the next card cheaply. Be aware of position and don't get trapped for a raise.

Improvement on fourth street is a key seven-card stud concept. If you don't improve on fourth street, and it looks like your oppo-nents did, then go ahead and give it up. The pot is still small and isn't worth taking any big risks.

FIFTH STREET: THE THIRD BETTING ROUND

Fifth street is usually decision time. Most of the hands you give up should be given up on either third or fifth street. By the fifth card, your hand will have either developed well enough to proceed to the river or not. If not, then fold.

Tactical Considerations on Fifth Street

You should usually be at least a little concerned if your opponent pairs his door card. This is particularly true if it's a big card. The reason, of course, is that his hand may have improved dramatically, there's some chance he's made trips, and if it's a big card there's a very good chance he's made either trips or a big two pair.

But don't always just assume he's made trips. Usually, he hasn't improved that much. If you know for sure he started with a pair, then it's a little better than even money that pairing his door card gives him trips, but that's only if you know for sure. If you factor in the chance that he started with some other hand, like three to a straight flush, then pairing the door card is less than even money to have given him trips.

If a player starts out with a pair, then two-thirds of the time that pair will be his door card. That's because if you know he has a pair, then his cards can be (xy)x or (yx)x or (xx)y. Two-thirds of these cards have one of the pair as the door card. But if his door card pairs, you now have extra information and it becomes less likely that he started with the door card as his pair. If he has a 7 up, then seeing another 7 means there's one less card that could have been a downcard 7, making it more likely that his starting pair is completely hidden.

So, although a consideration, you don't need to always be afraid of trips when a door card pairs. One example where trips is very unlikely is when the bring-in hand pairs his door card. It's not likely he started with a pair, he had no choice in whether or not to play. The bring-in is a completely random hand in terms of whether or not he's likely to have trips. That he pairs his door card doesn't mean much other than that he now has a low pair. And, of course, it's a low card.

Another situation, which is less obvious, is when a player has called a raise on third street with a small or medium-sized card that pairs on fourth street. This player isn't likely to have made trips because it's more likely he would have called a raise with a flush draw, or maybe a larger hidden pair. You might be concerned about such a player having made two pair, but it's very unlikely he's made trips.

You aren't making a big mistake if you fold almost automatically when an opponent pairs a door card on fourth street. The reason it's not much of a mistake is that the pot is still small. But on fifth street, the pot has started to get a little bigger, and automatically folding when an opponent pairs his door card is a bigger mistake.

SIXTH STREET: THE FOURTH BETTING ROUND

Sixth street play should be fairly routine. If you're in the lead, you should be betting. If you aren't in the lead on fifth, then you should probably still be calling unless you made your hand with the sixth street card—then you should be raising.

If you've gotten to sixth street, you usually aren't going to be giving up. The pot will have gotten big enough so that you need to be very sure that you're beat, or drawing dead, to give up at this point.

For example, in a recent hand I made a flush in the first five cards, betting the draw the whole way and betting the flush when I'd made it. On sixth street, my board looked like Q♣ J♣ 9♣ 2♠. I had bet the flush on fifth street even though both callers had paired, both of them pairing their door card. It seemed to me that my hand was likely to be a straight or a flush. But on sixth street, one of the players bet right out.

His board looked like 7♣ 4♠ 7♥ 8♣. When he caught that 8 and bet right into what I thought was an obvious full hand, I started to get worried. And it was not just my hand—the other active player had also paired his door card. (88)7 or (87)7 are exactly the kind of hands he might have started with. I was almost convinced he'd filled up and I was dead.

Almost. I was no longer certain I had the best hand. But the pot had gotten pretty big, so I called. I called again on the river. He'd made 8s and 7s, a weak two pair, and was just oblivious to what anybody else might have.

You'll run into that a lot in low-limit stud games. Many players in these games simply pay no attention at all to other players' hands. They play their own hand and if they make two pair they bet. That's as far as their thinking goes. When you run into this situation, you just have to suck it up and call.

I didn't think I had the best hand. But, usually, by the time you get to sixth or seventh street, the pot is large enough to call even if you probably don't have the best hand. When the pot is laying you 10-1, then even if your call loses 80 percent of the time, the call shows a meaningful long-term profit.

SEVENTH STREET: THE FINAL BETTING ROUND

By the river, the pot is usually big enough to make it worth calling with as little as a pair. This means it's big enough to make it worth it to your opponent to call with as little as a pair. When this is the situation, you can often make some pretty thin value bets.

I made a recent very thin value bet with nothing but a pair of Kings. I was called and won. He had a pair of 4s.

I'd been betting the whole way, and on the river my board was A♦ J♣ 6♣ 9♦. My pair of Kings were buried. It probably looked like a busted straight draw to him. His board was K♥ 10♣ 2♥ 6♠. I had his King blocked pretty well, and I had one of his 6s. I just didn't think he had two pair, and if he did have a King I had him out kicked. I don't recommend that thin of a bet all of the time— probably most of the time you shouldn't make that bet. But this time it worked out. Some players will often call with a small pair, others will seldom make that call. It just depends on what you know about the habits and tendencies of the other players.

Against most players he's probably much more likely to call or raise with two pair or trips than he is to call with just one pair. If you don't have specific knowledge of the player that suggests to you he's likely to call with just a pair, then it would probably be best to just check and show it down.

But sometimes the players in low-limit stud games are so soft that their being in the game is enough to suggest they'll call with less than Kings. Sometimes, it just gets downright goofy. When it does, you sometimes need to stretch a little bit and make some of those thin bets.

GENERAL COMMENTS ON THE GAME

Seven-card stud is a game of live cards. You have to be alert to other players' upcards, not just how it might effect their hand, but also how it effects your hand.

Every betting round brings a new set of upcards and a new situation.

Use the upcards and your opponents' actions to put them on a hand. Does he have a straight draw? A flush draw?

Many players will bet automatically if they have three cards to a flush showing, trying to represent a hand they don't have. A corollary to this is that a player who is aggressive with a completely uncoordinated board and has no possible straight or flush is probably not bluffing. He isn't representing anything, so he probably has a hand.

BOOKS ON SEVEN-CARD STUD

Seven-card stud isn't as popular as hold'em and, as a result, there aren't as many good books on stud as on hold'em. But there are a few. Probably the most popular is Roy West's *Seven Card Stud: The Complete Course in Winning at the Low and Medium Limits* (1996). West writes a regular column for *Card Player* magazine and preaches tight play and patience—exactly what you need to beat low-limit seven-card stud. The book is a little pricey, but it's pretty solid.

Another decent introduction for a novice stud player is Paul Kammen's *How to Beat Low Limit 7 Card Stud Poker* (2003). It provides some solid tips and beginning advice.

David Sklansky, Mason Malmuth, and Ray Zee, in *Seven-Card Stud for Advanced Players* (1999), exclusively cover high-ante, structured-betting seven-card stud games. An example of structured betting is a game with a $15 limit on third and fourth street, and a $30 limit on fifth, sixth, and seventh street. The bet doubles on fifth street. Such games tend to lend themselves to more tactical ploys related to bet size and this book puts a lot of emphasis on deception and fancy play, rather than the straightforward play that gets the money in the typical no-ante, spread-limit game. The book is very pricey and not really appropriate for the vast majority of casino seven-card stud games.

The newest seven-card stud book on the market is Ashley Adams's *Winning 7-Card Stud* (2003). The book focuses on taking home-game players, losing casino players, and hold'em players and turning them, step by step, into winning stud players. About two-thirds of the book is devoted to the low-limit stud games, and the last third concentrates on midlimit structured games. It's probably the most complete seven-card stud book on the market.

4

Omaha

Omaha is usually played as a hi/lo split game. But, it's also sometimes played as a regular high-only version. The high-only version of Omaha isn't played in many cardrooms. It's very popular in the New Orleans area for some reason, but it's not as often spread in other parts of the country. Regardless, I think it's a worthwhile game to learn, or at least to learn the rudiments of. It's a game that easily illustrates a lot of fundamental concepts and that almost no one plays well.

I'm not sure where it comes from, but there is a perception among many players that you can play more hands in Omaha than you can in hold'em. This perception is false. It is true that you can play more hands in loose games than in tight games. And, where Omaha games are frequently spread, it seems that the game is often very loose. But the inherent character of Omaha is that, everything else being equal, you should play fewer hands in Omaha than in hold'em. The beauty of Omaha is that everything else is seldom equal. Yes, Omaha games tend to be loose. And, yes, you can play more hands in a loose Omaha game than you would in a tight hold'em game. But this is because of the difference between loose and tight games, not because of a difference between Omaha and hold'em.

As a general rule, the more cards of your hand that you've seen, the tighter you should play. In Omaha, you're going to see nine cards in total, and at the first betting round you've seen four of them. You've only seen two cards that you're going to use in your final five-card hand, but you don't know which two they are. You've seen four out of nine. If those four don't all work together, you give it up right away. It is much less likely to get four out of four working together than two out of two in hold'em. So playing well, you should play fewer hands in Omaha than you would in a comparable hold'em game.

But there is a widely held fallacy that you should play looser in Omaha. It tends to make most Omaha games very loose games. This creates many opportunities to exploit the mistakes of others. This is what winning poker is all about: exploiting the mistakes of others. When you have players playing way too loose, it's important to get in there and mix it up with them, but you just have to do this very carefully. You want to play more hands, but you don't want to play as many hands as they do.

GAME PROCEDURES

Like hold'em, Omaha uses a button to indicate a nominal dealer position. Also like hold'em, it's typically played with two blinds, a small blind and big blind, where the big blind is the size of the bet on the first two betting rounds, called the small bet. There are four betting rounds, and the bet size on the last two rounds are typically twice the small bet, called the river bet. Sometimes, the game is played with different betting limits, such as 4/8/12/16 or 4/4/8/12. But I'll mostly deal with the standard two-level structure of a small bet and big bet.

The Deal

Each player is dealt four cards in turn, which are their private cards. This is followed by a betting round. Before the hand is over, there will be five community cards face up on the table. Your poker hand will consist of the best five-card combination that can be made using exactly two of your private cards and three community cards. The betting round after the deal starts with the first player after the big blind and commences around in order to the big blind. If no one has raised, the big blind can either check or raise.

The Flop

Three cards are dealt face up in the middle of the table. These are community cards. There is another betting round. The betting round after the flop begins with the first player to the right of the button. This will be one of the blinds if the blinds still have active hands. Because of this early position in later betting rounds, the blinds should tend to play fairly tightly preflop.

The Turn

One more card is dealt face up in the middle of the table. It's followed by another betting round. The order of the betting round is the same as the order on the flop.

The River

The final card is dealt face up in the middle of the table, completing the five community cards. Then there's the final round of betting.

The Showdown

After the final betting round, the cards are shown down, and the best combination of two cards from the players' private hands and three from the board wins.

HAND VALUES IN OMAHA AND HAND SELECTION

The four cards of your starting Omaha game need to work to-gether—all of them. Hold'em players who play Omaha for the first time often make fundamental mistakes in evaluating the value of Omaha hands.

At first, they'll tend to think of their four-card Omaha hand as just two hold'em hands. So, if they get a hand like Q♣ Q♠ 8♦ 9♦, they think they have a good hand. After all, Q♣ Q♠ is a very good hold'em hand and 8♦ 9♦ is also a pretty good hold'em hand. But the combination is not a good Omaha hand. All of the cards need to work together, not just all combinations of two cards. This is the second mistake most hold'em players make in evaluating a starting Omaha hand: once they get over the idea of looking for two hold'em hands, they realize that there are six combinations of two cards in a four-card Omaha hand and they look for four cards that will make six good hold'em hands. The best example of a terrible Omaha hand that makes six very good hold'em hands is four Aces.

Four big straight cards are an example of what I mean by work-ing together. Hands like K♠ Q♣ J♥ 10♦ or A♠ K♣ Q♥ J♦ can be good hands. If they hit the right flop, you'll have a hand like the top two pair plus a nut straight draw. The best hand and the best draw is about as much as you can hope for in Omaha. These are the kinds of hands that can turn into that. They are good hands that can become very powerful with the right flop.

It helps if those hands are suited, giving you flush draw potential on top of the straight potential. When the hands are suited, you re-ally want a card suited with the Ace, because you don't want to end up making a second-best flush. Second-best flushes are common in this game and can be very expensive. So A♠ K♣ Q♥ J♠ is much stronger than A♠ K♣ Q♥ J♥ and A♠ K♣ Q♥ J♥ isn't much stronger than A♠ K♣ Q♥ J♦. Having a potential for a flush draw counts for a little, but having a potential nut-flush draw counts for a lot.

You do want a possibility of hitting a hand in multiple ways. So a hand like Q♠ Q♣ J♥ 10♥ is much better than a hand like Q♠ Q♥ J♥ J♣. With the two pairs, you might flop a set or you might flop a nut straight draw, but you won't flop both. You might flop a set and a straight draw, but only if there are three to a straight on the board, making any straight draw you might have very vulnerable. With the one pair and the two adjacent straight cards, you might flop a set or you might flop a nut straight draw, but you might also flop both. And flopping both is what you need to have a very strong flop.

You don't have to have four broadway cards to have a good hand. And pairs can work with other cards also. But you do want straight cards, usually no more than one pair, and flush cards. If they aren't big cards, you probably want to avoid the hands from early position and you don't want to cold call a raise. A hand like 9♠ 9♣ 8♠ 7♣ can be very strong. But it's usually not a strong holding for early position. The suited nature of this hand is a positive attribute, but don't make the mistake of putting too much weight on it. The flop you're really looking for is a top set with a straight draw. A flush draw with it is a nice backup, but anything less than a nut flush isn't your primary goal.

PLAYING THE FLOP

Most of the opportunities for exploitation of the mistakes of others comes from errors made on the play of the flop. Omaha is all about flopping strong draws. This is counterintuitive to many poker players who think of a good start in terms of starting with a made hand rather than with a draw. If you flop a straight with no redraws, then you probably don't have a good hand in Omaha. An example of a redraw is a hand of 9♠ 8♥ 7♥ 6♣, and a flop of 5♠ 4♥ 3♥ or 7♠ 6♥ 5♥. In the both cases, you've flopped a straight, and in the first case you'll still have a nut straight should a 9, 8, 7, or 6 fall. In the second case, you have the top two pair in addition to the straight, so you'll have a high full house should a 7 or 6 fall. In both cases, you have a flush draw in addition to the straight, but the redraw doesn't add much value. You have the nut straight, you really don't want to make a flush.

The mathematics of draws in Omaha can get complex because you often have more than one draw, and some of your draws may be up against better draws (your 9 high flush may not be the best flush, and if you have a bottom two pair and make a full house, it might not be the best full house).

In most loose games, you'll want to see a lot of flops, but if all you flop is a draw, you usually should just give it up on the flop. Hands like the top set, likely to be the best hand, should be played very aggressively. Strong draws that are likely to make the nuts should also be played aggressively. Hands that are less than the nuts and draws to potentially second-best hands should be played more carefully.

The flop often gives you a few backdoor draws. These are draws where you have three to a straight or flush and need both of the final two cards to hit you in order to make your hand. By itself, a backdoor draw is close to worthless. But sometimes a combination of backdoor draws can be worth playing. This is not always an easy decision. You need to especially take into account your position relative to hands that haven't acted yet. The greater the chance that there might be a raise, the more you should tend toward folding hands that are mostly made up of backdoor draws.

A common belief about Omaha is that you should only play the nuts or a draw to the nuts. This isn't entirely true. While it's true that your primary draws should be to the nuts, draws to less than the nuts do have value. For example, a middle set with a flush draw, even if the flush draw isn't headed by an Ace, might be a good holding with a flop like 9♣ 8♥ 7♥. A hand like 8♥ 8♣ 6♥ 5♣ might be a pretty good holding for that flop. Your straight probably isn't any good, but it might be. If you fill up, you won't have the nuts but it will probably be good. And you have both a heart draw and a backdoor club draw. This hand has a lot of marginal value, and it has enough to add up to a fairly good hand, assuming that the action isn't real heavy on the flop. Against real heavy action there's a good chance you're drawing dead and you should probably give it up. This is the major reason hands like these shouldn't be played from early position. You don't want to hit a flop that you're unsure about and have to make a decision before other players have acted and given you information about their strength.

Playing draws on the flop is key in this game. You can have wrap straight draws with as many as twenty or so outs to the nuts. Such draws are very powerful and should be played very aggressively on the flop. Powerful multiway draws are often much better hands on the flop than a made hand.

Made hands without redraws can be worth a call but often shouldn't be played really aggressively. Something like 8♥ 9♦ 10♦ 10♥ with a flop of 6♣ 7♣ 8♠ is an example of a made hand that you probably don't want to get aggressive with on the flop, but that you also don't want to give up on. You have the nuts, but a lot of cards can beat you. Call and see how things progress on the turn.

PLAYING THE TURN

On the turn, you'll often want to give up on hands you played aggressively on the flop or get aggressive with hands you played passively on the flop. The turn card can destroy a solid draw.

If you hit the flop hard with a wrap straight draw and the turn card pairs the board, then you might have to just give it up if somebody else bets. It has just become too likely that you're drawing dead and that someone turned a full house. You don't need to automatically fold, but you should certainly give it serious consideration if the board pairs on the turn and anyone shows some aggression.

And a hand such as the nut straight with no redraws discussed earlier becomes much stronger if a blank hits the turn—strong enough to start playing very aggressively. On the flop, players with a lot of outs to draw at had two chances to hit and beat you. But if they clearly missed the turn, their chances of catching up to you have been severely reduced and you should respond with aggressive play.

A raise from another player on the turn usually means either the nuts or a draw to the nuts—often both.

PLAYING THE RIVER

Unless you have the nuts, the river is the time to slow down. Bluffs can work on the river, but probably won't. The likelihood is that someone has something and will call unless the board is very, very scary for them. The river is not the time to call a raise. Most players are very unlikely to raise on the river with anything less than the nuts.

SOME OBSERVATIONS ON OMAHA

Omaha isn't hold'em played with extra cards. The deal and betting progress in a similar way, but the games are very different in the way you should be thinking about the game. Hold'em is very much a game of big cards, seven-card stud is a game of live cards, and Omaha is a game of big draws.

Betting Structure

The betting structure matters a lot in Omaha. When it's played with escalating limits, like 3/6/9/12, the value of draws goes up a lot. You have implied odds with draws because the bet on the flop is small compared to the bet you can make later if you make the draw. When you're playing Omaha with escalating bet sizes, you should sometimes give up on the flop with the nuts. For example, if you have something like A♣ A♠ 6♣ 7♠ and flop 5♥ 4♥ 3♦, you have the nuts but no way to improve. Any heart, 6, 7, 5, 4, 3 might give another player a better hand. A diamond isn't a good card for you. If there's a lot of action, like maybe a bet, a raise, and a call in front of you, you might just want to dump a hand like that in a game with escalating bet sizes. I'm not saying you should automatically dump it, but there are times where you should give serious consideration to dumping the nuts with no redraws on the flop.

Freerolling in Omaha

Freerolling is when two players have the best hand on an intermediate betting round but one also has a draw to a better hand. Typically, freerolling occurs when two players have a straight and one has a flush draw or a set (giving him a strong full house draw). It's a situation that occurs often in Omaha, so you should often back off from heavy reraising with the nuts on intermediate betting rounds unless you're the one freerolling.

Playing Too Many Hands

You usually want to see a lot of flops in Omaha—but you don't want to see them all. It's easy for a player to fall into a trap of seeing value in hands that don't really have much value. 9♠ 9♣ 6♥ 6♠ is not much of a hand. But after a while, it can start to look like a good hand to some players. Don't let yourself fall into this trap. Look for a hand with all the cards working together and that has the potential of flopping both the nuts and a draw to an improvement.

One of the reasons that Omaha isn't spread in most cardrooms is because it's so easy to fall into the trap of playing very, very poorly. Seeing too many flops and chasing weak draws can be deadly. And the games quickly dry up, with the weakest players losing their money very quickly. Bad players have many opportunities to make mistakes in Omaha, more so than in games like hold'em or stud, and when they take advantage of these opportunities, they will go bust almost certainly.

Don't play every hand. Don't play with small sets and bottom two pair that are likely to make a second-best full house. Don't draw to less than a nut straight. Don't draw to baby flushes. Keep yourself out of trouble. Don't draw to a flush if the board is paired. Don't draw to a straight if the board has a flush draw. Proceed carefully. If you follow these general guidelines, it will be hard to lose at Omaha against most competition.

5

Hi/Lo Split Games

Any poker variant can be played as hi/lo split—the high hand gets half the pot and the low hand gets half. But some forms of poker seem to lend themselves more to hi/lo split than others. The most common hi/lo split games played in public cardrooms are Omaha hi/lo split and seven-card stud hi/lo split. The most popular casino game, hold'em, is almost never played hi/lo split. A few years ago, some casinos did offer a hi/lo split hold'em, but it never caught on, and I don't think it's spread anywhere today. Hi/lo split hold'em just doesn't seem to work. But Omaha and seven-card stud make good hi/lo games. In the case of Omaha, the game is even more popular when played hi/lo than it is when played high only.

Hi/lo split in a casino is typically played with an 8 qualifier for low—you can't win the low half without an 8 low or better. This means you have five unpaired cards with no card higher than an 8. An A2478 or 23456 is a low hand, but 22356 or 23459 are not low hands.

The reason for the 8 qualifier is primarily to speed up the game. It takes time to split up the pot and the cardroom gets its fee by raking each pot. The more pots, the more rake. Without the qualifier, every pot has to be split, which takes up time and gives fewer pots and smaller rake.

Because of this, some cardrooms simply refuse to spread hi/lo split games. The only time you'll see a hi/lo split game without the qualifier spread is probably going to be in a high-limit or pot-limit game that collects a time charge from each player rather than a rake.

The standard rule for low hands is the California loball rules, where straights and flushes don't count against a low hand—the best low is A2345. Aces can play as both high and low—AA is both the highest pair and the lowest pair. You may run across other rules for defining lows. If straights and flushes do count against a low hand, and Aces count only high, the best low is 75432 of at least two different suits. This is sometimes called deuce-to-seven loball or Kansas City loball, although I'm pretty sure cardrooms in Kansas City follow California loball rules.

You'll sometimes find different rules for what constitutes a low in home games, rules such as straights and flushes count against a low and Aces go both ways, or Aces are always high but straights and flushes don't count. In rare low-only games in cardrooms (like five-card loball draw or seven-card razz), you'll also sometimes find variations on the rules for a low hand. But cardroom rules for low in hi/lo split games are fairly standard. There may be some exceptions somewhere, but I'm not aware of them. Straights and flushes don't count against a low hand and Aces can be played high and low. A wheel (5 high straight) is the nut low in most games.

If no hand meets the 8 qualifier for low, then the high hand gets the whole pot. You might sometimes find a seven-card stud hi/lo that has a qualifier for high also, and some games are played with a two-pair qualifier for high. But this is rare and I don't address this variation in this book.

In a hi/lo game, you form two separate hands, one for the low and one for the high. You don't have to use the same five cards for your high hand as you do for your low hand. They can be the same hand. You don't have to declare whether you're going for high or low: just turn your hand face up and let the cards speak for themselves as to whether you have a low hand or a high hand, or both.

HI/LO SPLIT PRINCIPLES

Frequent split pots in hi/lo split games do make these games different from regular, high-only poker games. Some strategic situations are enhanced in hi/lo split games.

In regular forms of poker, you're always going for all the pot, and any extra consideration involving a draw for half the pot seldom arises. In hi/lo split games, you're still interested in the whole pot, but you'll frequently run into situations where you're probably going to have to settle for half. Sometimes, you can even get a piece of the pot and lose money.

Key cards are also more common in hi/lo split games.

Scooping

A critical principle of playing hi/lo split games is to play for the whole pot. Winning half the pot can be a nice consolation prize, and if the pot is contested multiway, then getting just half the pot can even be profitable. Getting half the pot when you contributed one-third is slightly profitable for you. But it's not a road to riches and it's not your primary goal. Winning the whole pot is called scooping and a scoop should be your goal in every pot you play. You don't want to draw for a chance at half the pot, you do not want to chase in the hopes you just get your money back. If you don't have decent prospects for a scoop, then just don't play.

Since hi/lo split games in casinos are played with a qualifier, requiring 8-low or better to qualify as a low hand, sometimes no one will have a low and there won't be a split pot. Generally, there are two direct ways to scoop: win the high end when no one has a qualifying low or win both the high and low ends. But there's also a third way to scoop: having everyone else fold without a showdown. You can often scoop this third way when you have half the pot locked up, with a nut low or nut high, and play very aggressively. When you have half the pot locked up, you can often just use aggression to dissuade an opponent with a weak hand from trying to compete for the other half. If he doesn't call, you win. This situation tends to arise more often when you have a low hand for two reasons. One is that nut lows are easier to make than nut highs and the other is because when you have the nut low, it's not as likely someone has a draw to the nut high as it is that someone has a draw to the nut low when you have the nut high.

Because of this potential for a low-only hand to scoop, hands that really only have low potential do have scoop potential. Aggression goes a long way.

You don't just win twice as much when you scoop. The pot you win is twice the size because the amount you contribute is the same whether you get half or all of the pot; the amount you win is significantly more than twice as much. Except in rare heads up situations, the amount of the pot that you've contributed is much less than half.

There's a little more risk in playing a hand that only has a chance to win the high, because you're gambling that no other player will make a low. So most of the time you'll want to be playing hands that have chances to win both ways—two-way hands that can win both high and low.

Key Cards

In most forms of hi/lo split, Aces are key cards. Aces are part of nut lows, of top pair, nut flushes, and of broadway straights. Aces are key cards because they are critical in making a variety of nut hands. They are also important in scoops. They are very important cards, so having them not only gives you all these possibilities, but they also deny the card to the other players. A pair of Aces is very powerful in a hi/lo split, partly because this means half the Aces aren't held by your opponents.

Freerolling

Freerolling occurs frequently in hi/lo split games. Often, you'll have the low side locked up with the nut low and will be freerolling with a draw to a high for the other half of the pot.

The freeroll concept is where a lot of the value of suited Aces comes from. If you start out with an Ace and a suited baby card, you'll often make a low and have a flush draw backup. This can be a powerful holding.

SEVEN-CARD STUD HI/LO SPLIT

Seven-card stud hi/lo split is a seven-card stud variation where the high hand and the low hand split the pot.

Game Procedure

The playing procedure of seven-card stud hi/lo split follows the procedure of seven-card stud. The only difference in procedure is at the showdown, where if there is a qualifying low hand the pot is split.

Depending on the cardroom, there might also be a difference in the betting structure. While most low-limit seven-card stud games have no ante and use a spread limit of $1 to $5, hi/lo split is more likely to be spread with structured limits. A 3/6 game might have a fifty-cent ante, the low card must bring it in for at least a $1, and all bets after the initial bringing are $3 on third and fourth streets, and $6 on fifth, sixth, and seventh streets. Some cardrooms might still spread seven-card hi/lo split as a spread-limit game though. It just depends on where you are and what the players want.

Most of what follows is intended for the spread-limit variety, but for the most part it is also applicable to the structured game. At the end of the seven-card discussion, I give a few comments on how the structured limits change things somewhat.

THIRD STREET: HAND SELECTION AND THE FIRST BETTING ROUND

As I said before, stick with hands that have multiple ways to win. Generally, this means low hands with some kind of high potential (straight draw, flush draw, or an Ace).

Every hand has a high hand winner, but not every hand has a low winner—often, no one makes an 8 or lower hand. So since you never want to be stuck drawing for half the pot, avoid hands with only a low potential. A hand like (7♥ 2♣) 8♦ is a very weak hand in hi/lo split.

Sometimes, the difference can be subtle. (7♥ 2♣) 3♦ is an example of a weak start in seven-card stud hi/lo. Compare this to (7♥ A♥) 3♦. Now pairing the Ace or catching a third heart on fourth street will give you some chance at a high hand. Even better would be (A♥ 2♥) 3♦, with the added straight possibility plus the nut low. Play for the whole pot, not just for the crumbs

Hands like (A♥ 3♥) 3♦ usually aren't worth pursuing, unless you can get in for the minimum from late position and 2s, 4s, and 5s are live cards. A hand like this has a little bit toward a lot of ends: two to a flush, small pair with good kicker, or two to a low. But it's not enough for any of them. Wait for a solid start, not a lot of weak possibilities. In a game with antes, where the pot has more money to draw to, hands like this are worth pursuing for one bet to see if it develops, but in a no-ante game the pot just isn't big enough to make it worthwhile unless the circumstances are perfect.

The really powerful starts are three suited wheel cards headed by an Ace that's hidden. Deception is important in seven-card stud hi/lo.

Since every hand has a high winner (but not all hands have a low), the intuition of many players is that a high-hand start is a good start. In seven-card stud hi/lo, this intuition just doesn't match up with reality. A high-only start is almost always a losing proposition.

Big pairs too often end up getting beat by a low hand that backs into two pair or a flush. A pair of Kings is not a good start in seven-card hi/lo split.

The only big pair usually worth playing is Aces, and then only when the third card is a baby card. This is because the two Aces in your hand help block other players' low potential, and a low card to go with them gives you some low potential.

Three-card flush draws are generally only worth pursuing when you have an Ace with at least one baby card to go with it. Because a lot of players drawing for low can back into a flush, you don't want to be drawing for a second-best flush. And a low without an Ace is often a second-best low. Draw for the best, not for the second best. In late position in an unraised pot, you can often call on third street with only three low cards to a flush, without an Ace. But it's a weak start.

Your upcard should also be a consideration in deciding whether or not to play. There are occasions when you might want to limp in with a draw to an 8 low, but if the 8 is your door card, you should pass. It's one thing to have weakness, but it's another thing entirely to have weakness that is on display for everyone to see. Also, an 8 low is a weak hand.

One of the keys to scooping is getting them to give up the pot without a fight. Catching scare cards helps you to accomplish this. If they see you with three wheel cards showing, they'll often give up their high pairs, conceding the pot to you because they fear a wheel.

Three-card straights can be good hands to start with in the right circumstances. The smaller the starting straight, the better the hand. Wheel draws like a 345, especially if you have a two flush, can be very good starts if you have good position and aren't likely to be raised. It's important to get in cheaply with these marginal hands that can potentially develop into something. If they don't develop on fourth street, dump the hand and try again next time.

In a typical, loose game, you don't want to even start with most hands that only have a chance to win the high half. The only exceptions would be trips or a pair of Aces. Even a pair of Aces should probably have a suited card or a baby card to go along with it (preferably a wheel card suited with one of the Aces). If there's a lot of raising going on at third street, you'll want to muck most Ace pairs. The reason is that with a lot of action there is a good chance that your Aces aren't live.

One hand that a lot of loose players think of as a potential scoop hand is (A♣ 2♣) K♥. The thinking is that it has both big cards and little cards, so it has prospects both ways. This thinking is very wrong headed. In some circumstances, when the opponents are very loose and very passive, the hand might have some value because of the deceptive value if you do get very lucky and catch a low. But it does require you to get very lucky. You do rely on the idea of getting lucky somewhat when you're playing poker. But the idea is to put yourself in a position where you have a lot of ways to get lucky, not where luck is all you have going for you.

(A♣ 2♣) K♥ has a weak start either way, but not both ways. The only chance it has both ways is the two-card low and the two-card flush. Face cards are often called "bricks" in hi/lo games. There's a reason for this.

In tight games, high hands can sometimes scoop against a single opponent. But if you're in such a game, the best thing to do is probably just find a better game. High-only hands are not a strong prospect to get the money in most games, and if the game is tight enough to give high hands any meaningful equity, there isn't much money to get anyway.

Fourth Street: The Second Betting Round

Fourth street is a critical decision point in seven-card hi/lo split. You want to improve on fourth street if you're going to continue the hand. Ideally, you want to catch a low card that doesn't pair you and that continues either a flush draw or straight draw. Of course, you usually won't hit the ideal. But when you do, get aggressive. Strong two-way draws are very strong hands in hi/lo split poker. This is especially true in seven-card stud if you have a threatening board in addition to strong draws.

Sometimes any improvement, even marginal improvement, is enough to continue, and sometimes you want to look for a strong improvement. How you should play your hand on fourth street depends mostly on the size of the pot—on whether it was raised or not on third street. If the pot has been raised, it's usually big enough to justify chasing some. I tend to let the other players have the little pots, while I go after the big pots aggressively. With a large pot, just a little bit of an improvement is enough to take off another card.

When There Was a Third Street Raise. If there was a third street raise, the pot is often large enough to make it worth chasing for one more card, even if fourth street only gives you minor improvement. If you're in good position, and there isn't heavy action on fourth street, an improvement as minor as catching a K♣ when you started with (A♣2♣) 5♦ might be enough.

Strong improvement on fourth street when there has been a third street raise usually calls for aggressive action. With the same start as above, catching a 4♣ gives you a very powerful draw and you should probably get every bet you can in on fourth street. Bet it and if you get raised, reraise. If possible, it's important to structure your aggression in such a way as to trap mediocre draws in between you and another apparently strong hand. You structure this aggression by either betting or check-raising, depending on the relative position of the other source of aggression.

When There Was No Third Street Raise. There is an old adage that comes from no-limit poker but still has application here: "Don't go busted in an unraised pot." If the pot is still small, and you only have marginal improvement, don't bother continuing. In an unraised pot, you'll usually only want to continue if you improved in both your high and low chances. You want to have started out with a low draw and had the fourth street card be a low card that moved you closer to a straight or flush. This is a general idea that applies to almost all forms of poker: Don't aggressively go after small pots, let the other players have the little ones. Save your efforts for the big ones, which are worth an aggressive pursuit.

An exception would be when you improve against an opponent who appears to have not improved.

If you start out with three babies and pair one of your downcards, while an opponent who has a low card in the door catches a brick, then a bet from you will often cause them to fold. It looks like your hand is improving to a solid low while his hand is going backward. Most players will simply give it up in this situation when the pot is small.

Fifth Street: The Third Betting Round

Generally, if you call a bet on fifth street you should be expecting to go to the river with it. This is not always the case, because things can sometimes really turn sour on sixth street. And much of the idea about a call on fifth street committing you to the river comes from higher-limit games when the bet sizes are fixed and structured, with the bet doubling on fifth street.

If you have a very strong low draw on fifth street, it's a good time to be getting aggressive. How low your cards need to be to have a strong low draw depends on

- How small the exposed cards of your opponent are
- How threatening your exposed cards are
- How live your cards are
- And, to a lesser extent, how dead your opponents cards are

Something like 2♣ 3♣ 4♣ exposed in your upcards can appear very threatening. You should usually play a threatening board aggressively, even if you don't have a made hand. Sometimes, what you have isn't as important as what they think you have.

Sixth Street: The Fourth Betting Round

Sixth street play is fairly automatic. Bet when you think you have the best hand, call when you think you have a good draw. If you've been pushing a low draw up to this point, now is probably the time to stop.

Seventh Street: The Final Betting Round

Sometimes, you should call with as little as a small pair. When an obvious low bets the river and no obvious high has called, any pair is sometimes enough to get the high. Two pair on the river is an almost automatic call.

If your hand is concealed (low hand looks like a high hand or high hand looks like a low hand), you should almost always be betting. Betting a low hand with a board of 7♣ 8♣ 9♣ 10♣ will often result in players with just a pair for high to fold. The key to exploiting any advantage you have from a concealed hand is to bet the hand if it's the one they think it is, not as if it's the hand it actually is.

Playing Aces in Seven-Stud Hi/Lo Split

Generally, you shouldn't chase high-only hands. The one exception is a pair of Aces. A pair of Aces is probably the best start for high and your having two of the Aces cuts off a lot of the low-draw competition. Some of your opponents won't draw to a low without an Ace in their hand and the ones who do will be drawing thinner than they think. When you start out with a pair of Aces in your first three cards, there are two things you need to consider before you act: whether the Aces are concealed and whether the odd card gives you a backdoor low (it's also of interest whether the odd card gives you a two flush, but that's not as important as the other two considerations).

Just to give you an idea about how a lone pair of Aces fares heads up against a weak low draw, a (9♠ A♣) A♦ has 53 percent pot equity against a (7♥ 4♥) 2♥. Add the value you'll get if you have a two flush, or if the 9 is a baby card, and the tactical value of deception that might convince another hand not to draw against you, and a pair of Aces can be a pretty good start. (3♣ A♣) A♦ has 58 percent pot equity against the (7♥ 4♥) 2♥. This is a pretty solid edge.

The difference in tactical advantage from having a hand like (A♣A♦) 9♠ rather than (K♣ K♦) 9♠ is huge. With the Kings, if an opponent catches an Ace at some point, you have to be concerned that your Kings are beat. This is less likely to happen when you have two Aces, and even if it does happen it's not likely he made a pair of Aces when you have two of them.

Aces with a Small Card. If you have a small card with your pair of Aces, you have a decent chance for low. You'll have to catch good on both the next two cards, but even when you don't catch good you've got that pair, and if you have Aces up on fifth street, you might still back into a low hand. Unless the action is heavy, Aces up is probably going to be good enough for half the pot and it might scoop it. You don't want to draw for half the pot, but it's certainly okay to take half the pot when you can. When you start out with that pair of Aces, they are the ones drawing against you, and having a low card just gives you a potential redraw as a backup.

Open Aces with a Big Card. The strength of open Aces with a hidden big card is that the weakness of your hand is completely disguised. If you make two pair, no one will suspect it, as most will think you caught a brick. If you pick up a baby card, your opponents will fear a wheel draw (and you might even backdoor a wheel). If your hand is not developing nicely by fifth street, don't be afraid to give it up against what looks like a made low. By developing nicely, I mean picking up a flush draw and backdoor low, or making trips or Aces up. Unless the pot gets very large, it probably isn't worth going past fifth street with Aces only.

Deception is always worth something and in hi/lo split games deception is sometimes worth a lot.

Concealed Aces with a Big Card. The strength of concealed Aces is, of course, that they're concealed. But having a big card showing will suggest the likelihood that you have a big pair, so it's unlikely that the deception of the hidden pair will go very far for you. Concealed Aces with a big card showing is probably the weakest combination for starting Aces. Unless you get heads up against a draw, you want to make Aces up quickly to continue this hand. If it looks like you have bad position, or if it looks like there might be three or more low draws competing, you might want to give up on this combination from the outset. As I mentioned previously, a lot of low draws suggests that your Aces aren't live, and drawing for cards that aren't live is sure death in any form of seven-card stud.

Against a single low hand, unimproved Aces might be enough to take half the pot, so you'll often have to go into a check and call mode toward the end. Be careful that you're not getting into a situation where you're drawing dead against a made straight though.

General Comments on Seven-Card Stud Hi/Lo

Perceptions and deception are very important in seven-card stud hi/lo. Play your hand the way your opponents likely expect you to play it. If you have (A♣ 3♦)7♥ 4♥ 3♥, play it like you have a made low and a flush, not like a pair and a low draw. If you have (A♣ A♦)4♥ 3♥, play it like a wheel straight flush draw, not like a pair and a backdoor low. It's often very easy to convince them that you have the hand they're afraid you have. Making them believe that will often give you the whole pot when you only have the hand for half the pot.

A strong low draw is important in seven-card stud hi/lo and when you add some variations on betting, like structured betting or doubling the bet on the river, the importance of a strong draw is even greater.

Structured Betting. When the betting is structured rather than spread limit, the bet size doubles on fifth street. When this happens, the adage I mentioned earlier, that you shouldn't call a bet on fifth street unless you're committed to seeing the river, applies strongly. Don't pay a double sized bet to just take off "one more card." You either have a hand that's worth pursuing or you don't. If you don't, then just fold.

Appearance Matters. Much of the strength of your hand comes from appearance, from what your upcards look like. This is why a hand with an 8 as your door card is a weak start. There are no cards you can catch to dissuade other low draws from playing, because they know you're drawing to an 8 and they have better draws.

I played a hand of seven-card stud hi/lo online recently that demonstrates the value of appearances. I had the bring in with (6♦ K♣) 4♥. Two players called, one with a 7♥, and one with a 10♣. It looked like I was against one low draw and one high hand. I didn't have much of anything, but on fourth street I caught a King, giving me what was probably the best high. On fourth street, the board looked like this:

```
(6♦ K♣)    4♥     K♦
(X X )    10♣     J♠
(X X )     7♥     7♣
```

It looked like I caught a brick. So I decided to play it that way. The pair of 7s checked, solidifying my guess that he was drawing to a low, and the high hand bet. He might have had a pair, maybe a straight draw, but I thought my Kings were best at that point. The apparent high hand might have had a straight draw, a flush draw, or a big pair. But I didn't think he could beat a pair of Kings. On the fifth, I caught an Ace:

```
(6♦ K♣)    4♥     K♦     A♦
(X X )    10♣     J♠     5♣
(X X )     7♥     7♣     2♣
```

Now the appearance was that the pair of 7's and I were in a race to draw to a low and he had a backup pair. I caught a perfect scare card on sixth street, a 5. Given the way I had played the hand to this point, it looked like I had made a strong low, possibly even a wheel.

```
(6♦ K♣)    4♥     K♦     A♦     5♥
(X X)     10♣     J♠     5♣     8♦
(X X)      7♥     7♣     2♣     J♦
```

I then bet when the pair of 7s checked. The apparent high hand called but the 7s folded. He was concerned that drawing to a 7 wasn't going to be good enough. My pair of Kings won the pot in a showdown.

The point of this example is that by playing my hand deceptively, I scooped a pot that I likely would have won half of had I played the Kings strongly. By seeming to play the hand naturally as the upcards developed, I convinced the only low draw to give it up. Often, in seven-card hi/lo split you should let appearance drive your action more than what your actual hand is. If you think carefully about what your opponents probably think about your hand, deceptive behavior naturally follows.

OMAHA HI/LO

Omaha hi/lo is rapidly becoming the most popular hi/lo split game. Like hold'em has replaced seven-card stud as the most commonly played poker variant, Omaha has replaced seven-card stud as the most commonly played hi/lo split variant.

Game Procedure

Procedurally, Omaha hi/lo split is played the same as Omaha. At the showdown, the pot is split between the high and low hands. You don't have to use the same cards for your high and low hand. If two or more hands tie for the low half (or the high half), they split that half equally.

Hand Selection: The First Betting Round

Omaha hi/lo split is really a pretty simple game. If you play coordinated cards with scoop potential and pay attention to position, then you'll win against most opposition.

In the high-only version of Omaha, we want starting hands that have all the cards working together. This is not really the case in Omaha/8. We do want the hand to be somewhat coordinated, but having the cards working together doesn't really do the trick. Hands like J♥ 10♣ 9♥ 8♣ have all the cards working together but aren't good Omaha hi/lo split hands. A hand like this doesn't really have any scoop potential. Its prospects for high involve weak flush draws and straight draws that are likely to put low cards on the board, thereby increasing the chances you'll split the pot at best.

A hand like A♥ 2♥ K♣ K♦ doesn't have all the cards working together but is somewhat well coordinated for scoop potential. It has a potential for a nut flush, a nut low, and a nut straight. You don't want to make second-best hands in this game.

Like stud hi/lo, high pairs by themselves aren't worth fooling with. A hand like KKxx is generally not much of a hand. KK with a couple of low cards is worth playing from late position at times, but generally it's a clear fold unless the two low cards are wheel cards and it helps if one of them is an Ace. Suited helps also but not a lot, unless it's a suited Ace. A hand like K♥ K♦ 3♣ 7♠ isn't much of a poker hand. Pairs don't make for good Omaha/8 hands. AA with two broadway cards or two wheel cards is a strong exception.

Some hands with big pairs that can sometimes be worth playing include hands like K♥ K♣ A♦ 2♣, K♥ K♣ A♦ 3♣, K♥ K♣ Q♦J♣, K♥ K♣ Q♦ Q♣, and variations of these hands. A pair of Kings is a fairly decent hand when it's combined with an otherwise strong holding.

The ideal situation is late position and no raise. I'd also suggest against playing the hand after a tight player limps in from early position. You don't want to play the hand against an AA or A2.

The concept of a playable hand is one I'll get into in more depth later, but for most hands it depends on the situation more than the hand. K♥ K♣ 3♥ 2♣ is a playable hand, but if you start playing it from early position, if cold calling raises with it, or if calling a tight early position limpers with it, you'll go broke.

Steve Badger, a poker pro from California who plays mostly Omaha/8, likes K♥ K♣ 3♥ 2♣, which is a hand that really should only be played situationally. A pair of Kings can sometimes be played because it does have good scoop potential with the right companion cards. An A2 works well with a pair of Kings and so does a 23. If an Ace does flop, then you probably have a good low draw. If no Ace flops, the high pair has a good shot at high, or at least that's what Badger claims. I'm not sure I buy that myself.

Suited low draws, wheel cards, and broadway cards are good

starts. Avoid hands like K♥ K♠ 7♦ 3♣ or K♥ K♠ Q♦ 7♣. And play very tight from early position.

Hands to Avoid. Some hands with no possibility of making a low hand can scoop the pot when the board does not have the possibility of a low. An example is a hand like A♥ A♦ K♥ Q♦.

But most hands that do not have low potential should be avoided. The characteristics of the kinds of hands without low potential that you should avoid is that they only figure to make the best high hand in situations where the board does contain a low possibility.

Your goal in Omaha hi/lo split is to win the entire pot, rather than half the pot. Of course, you'll often end up with only half the pot, but you should select your spots with the goal of winning the whole thing. Keeping that goal in mind, there are some common characteristics of hands that should be avoided:

- Hands with weak high potential combined with weak low potential should be avoided
- Hands with midranked cards should be avoided
- Hands that don't give you maximum potential by having all four cards working for you should be avoided

Hands with midrank cards are pretty much worthless in Omaha hi/lo split. An example is a hand like 7♥ 7♦ 9♥ 10♦.

Making three 7s puts at least one low card on the board. If it is the top set, then the board has three low cards and probably also has straight possibilities. Three 7s is very unlikely to scoop the pot and might not even be enough to win the high half. And the times this hand makes a straight, it will either be a straight that we have the bottom part of or it will be a straight that puts two or three low cards on the board, giving someone else a chance at half the pot. The chances of making a second-best high hand or a high hand that can only win half the pot makes the prospects of this hand fairly bleak.

Hands that contain cards that are not either the lowest four cards or the highest four cards should usually just be avoided.

Even a hand like A♦ K♥ 7♦ 7♥ is not a hand with good prospects.

A♦ K♥ Q♦ 6♥ is another example of a hand with limited potential. It's one that might be played from late position with no raise.

Playing the Flop: The Second Betting Round

You want to hit the flop and hit it hard. Forty cards are dealt to the players and most of the cards are accounted for. It's very likely the flop hit someone, and if that someone isn't you, then don't get involved.

But sometimes it can look like the flop hit you hard, but it's not as strong as you might think after only a superficial view. An example of a situation where you're strong enough to bet but probably not strong enough to get carried away with a lot of raising would be if you limped in from the big blind with K♦ K♣ Q♥ 5♦ and a flop of K♥ Q♦ 5♣. With this dangling 5 and no Ace, this isn't a hand you'd usually want to voluntarily put money in the pot to play, but sometimes you just have to go with what you have.

How hard did that flop hit you? You do have top set, with no possible straight, and only backdoor flush and low draws. But look ahead to the next card. You have one of the Queens and one of the 5s blocked. And if any other card falls, it puts either a possible straight on the board or a combination possible straight and low draw. Take a moment to look at that.

It's very likely you aren't going to like the next card. By all means, bet the hand, you're best at the moment. But if you get raised, don't get real carried away until you see the turn.

The Turn: The Third Betting Round

Think about that same hand, K♦ K♣ Q♥ 5♦ and a flop of K♥ Q♦ 5♣. Give a turn card of A♦. Now there's a couple of hands that have your set of Kings beat. Someone with a pair of Aces has a bigger set, and a straight is possible. You're no longer the nuts. You did pick up a flush draw, so you have plenty of outs on the off chance someone does have you beat. But now the board gives others a draw for low. Because of that low, it's important that you bet here—don't let them draw at you for free. Of course, if you bet and get raised, you probably won't like it much, but you do have the flush draw to fall back on (and a full house draw). This bet should be pretty automatic.

The River: The Final Betting Round

This is where playing tight and carefully on early betting rounds pays off. Hopefully, you won't still have a live hand on the river unless you actually have something. So a lot of the guesswork of whether to call a bet disappears.

You don't have to have the nuts to bet on the river, and you don't have to have a two-way hand. But one thing to keep in mind is that most of your opponents think they have to have the nuts to raise. But they only have to have the nuts one way. So you should often call raises without the nuts if you think you have the other side.

I don't have a lot of solid prescriptive advice about playing the river in Omaha hi/lo split. Usually, you should have a premium hand for at least one side of the pot to get involved on the river.

Hand reading is key to playing the river. At each betting round, you should have been forming a hypothesis about a range of possible hands for each player. Every bet or call should result in your reducing that range. Part of reading their hand involves reading your own hand.

Reading Your Hand

Your final hand in Omaha/8 consists of two cards from your four-card hand and three cards from the five cards on the board. A different combination of cards can be used to form a high hand and a low hand.

Reading an Omaha hand takes some practice. A good way to start is to focus first on the board, ignoring your four-card hand. Try to determine what the best possible hand is, the nuts. Then look at your hand to see if you have those cards. This is an easier way to begin learning how to read a hand because if you look at your hand first you have six different two-card combinations you'll have to consider. Focusing on the board helps direct you to considering only those two-card combinations that matter. It has the added benefit of helping you consider what hands your opponents might have.

Determining the Nuts: High Hands. When examining the board to identify the best possible hand, it's usually best to use a process of elimination, starting with looking for four-of-a-kind possibilities.

Step 1. If the board contains a pair then four-of-a-kind is possible. To determine whether this is the best possible hand, make sure the board does not contain three cards to a straight flush.

Step 2. If no pair is on the board, then the best possible hand is a flush if the board contains three cards of the same suit (unless a straight flush is possible). Anyone who has two cards of that suit in his hand has a flush.

Step 3. If the board contains any three-card combination where the difference between the highest and lowest cards of the three is no more than four ranks, then a straight is possible. A, 10, 6, and 8, for example. The most obvious straight possibility is when the three cards come from an adjacent sequence, 10, 9, 8, for example. With this sequence on the board, anyone with a QJ, J7, or 76 has a straight.

Step 4. Three of a kind is the highest possible hand if the board does not contain a pair, three to a flush, or three to a straight.

High hands are looking to scoop the pot by having the best high hand and there being no low hand.

For a low to be feasible, there must be three nonpaired cards, 8 or lower, on the board. With a board of A♥ 2♦ 9♣ 10♣ A♣, it's not possible for anyone to have a low hand. The high hand takes the whole pot. It scoops.

The best possible hand for this flop is four Aces. If you have a pair of Aces in your four-card hand, then you have four Aces with a 10 kicker.

With the flop above, if your hand is A♦ 3♣ 4♣ J♦, then you have a club flush, A♣ 10♣ 9♣ 4♣ 3♣.

Note that any other player who has two clubs will have a higher flush than you.

With a hand of A♦ 2♣ 4♣ J♦, you have a full house, A♥ A♦ A♣ 2♦ 2♣.

With a hand of J♣ 2♣ 4♦ J♦, you have two pair, Aces and Jacks, A♣ A♦ J♣ J♦ 10♥

Straights can sometimes be tricky to read. Remember, you have to use exactly two cards for your hand. If you have A♣ 6♣ K♥ K♦ and the board is K♣ 2♣ 3♥ 4♥ 5♠, then you do not have a straight. You have three kings. But with a hand of A♣ 2♦ K♥ K♦, you would have a 5-high straight, with a hand of 5♣ 6♣ K♥ K♦ you would have a 6-high straight.

Be sure to note that neither of these hands will make a full house since you cannot use three cards out of your hand.

When there are four cards in sequence on the board, it is very likely that someone has a straight. With the flop above, the nut high hand is a 7-high straight. Anyone with a 6, 7 has the nut high. But, other holdings that give a straight are A2; A3; A4; A5; 6, 2; 6, 3; 6, 4; 6, 5; or 6, 7.

Determining the Nuts: Low Hands. If the board contains three or more cards no higher than an 8, then a low hand is possible. If the board is A♣ 2♥ 3♦ 4♠ 5♥, then anyone who has two cards, 5 or lower, has a perfect low hand. But if your hand is K♥ Q♥ 6♠ 7♠, then you have only a 7-low, 7♠ 6♠ 3♦ 2♥ A♣. This is sometimes called 76123. Note that you've also got a 7-high straight, using the same two cards from your hand but a different three cards from the board.

If the board is A♣ 2♥ 3♦ 6♦ 7♥ and you have the above hand,

then you again have a 7-low. You would have the same low hand if your four-card hand had A♥ 3♣ 10♣ 10♥. A player with any of these cards on the board plus either a 4 or a 5 would have a better low.

Two-Way Hands. Every showdown in Omaha has a high hand. The highest hand at the showdown will take at least half the pot. Always.

A low hand, however, has to qualify. It must be at least an 8-low or better to qualify. So in order for there to be a low half of the pot, the board must contain at least three unpaired cards 8 or lower, and at least one active player must have two unpaired cards 8 or lower that do not match the three board cards. If there is no low, the high hand gets the entire pot.

Of course, it's possible for the same player to have both the best high and the best low hand. Sometimes, this is done by playing the same cards for high and for low.

For example, say your hand is A♠ 2♠ 4♦ 5♥ with a board of A♥ 2♥ 3♠ 9♠ 10♦. You have a perfect low hand and the same hand is also a straight, the best possible low and the highest possible straight.

With a board of 2♠ 6♠ 7♣ J♥ K♠, then any hand with A♠, any other spade, and any three would scoop with a nut low and a nut flush. An example would be A♠ 3♠ 4♥ 5♥.

General Comments on Omaha Hi/Lo

Getting Quartered. In Omaha hi/lo split, a big concern on the later streets is getting quartered for low. For a low to be possible, there must be three low cards on the board. These are community cards, so if a low is possible in a multiway pot, then a low is likely. And more than one player with the nut low is not at all uncommon. Two players tying for half the pot means they each get one-fourth, hence the term "getting quartered."

Of course, sometimes the high gets quartered, but it's more common on the low half.

Here's a hand where everybody involved made mistakes, including me. In this hand I was on the big blind with, among other cards, a 10 and a 5. There were five of us seeing the flop with a 10, 4, 5.

I had top two pair, but I got bad position and there were others competing for the pot. They almost certainly had low draws, so if I was lucky I'd end up with half the pot. I checked, the player on my left bet and got one caller, I went ahead and called.

Turn was a 10. Things just got a lot better for me, I now had the nut full house and any low draw just missed on one of his chances. I decided to get tricky and check. The bettor bet again, got a call, I raised. The bettor reraised. He got a call again, I just called.

The bettor obviously had a full house of some kind. The caller obviously had a low draw. I had the nuts. The other full house might have had me tied. But in previous hands he hadn't shown a clear sense of hand value. He could have 4s full of 10s with a backup low draw. At least that was what I was thinking at the time. But he could have had me tied with a low draw (I didn't have a low draw), so I slowed down.

The river was a 3. Okay, half the pot was gone. Was it worse? I didn't know. So, like a damn fool, I bet. The previous bettor raised and the caller reraised.

Oops. He had a 10, 5 and I was going to get quartered for high. I should not have bet the river.

I had the nut high, no low. The other full house had nut high, no low. And the low had nut low. I got one-fourth of the pot. The low draw who had been calling the whole way got half.

Counterfeited. I introduced the concept of being counterfeited in chapter 2. Counterfeiting is when the board duplicates a card already in your hand. It's an important consideration in Omaha hi/lo split. The very strongest hands are those that have protection from being counterfeited.

Lows often get counterfeited in Omaha hi/lo. A hand of A♥ 2♥ K♣ K♦ has its low counterfeited if a board of 8♠ 6♠ 3♦ Q♣ catches a 2♣ on the river. Now what had been the nut low is beat by a hand with an Ace and any live low card.

The implication is that the card may not be redundant for someone else and improve his hand.

If you have a bare Ace 2 low, catching an Ace or 2 is always a redundant card for you. Having a 3 or 4 to back up your low draw makes your hand much more powerful. A♥ 2♠ 3♣ 4♦ is a very powerful hand, primarily because of the counterfeit protection.

As in hold'em, straights are also easily counterfeited in Omaha hi/lo split.

A hand has a redraw when it's probably the best hand right now, but in case it's not, it has a draw to a better hand. The term "redraw" is often used in Omaha in situations where the term "outs" would be used in other poker variations. Having a redraw is important counterfeit protection in Omaha hi/lo split.

I played a hand recently that illustrates a counterfeited low hand. I played this hand terribly by the way.

I had an A♠ 2♥ 5♦ 7♣. Any hand that is an A2 is a pretty good hand, but this one wasn't all that great. The 7 didn't add much to the hand and it had no flush potential. I got a free look at the flop from the big blind, 3 hearts with a low draw K♥ 6♥ 8♥. The small blind checked, I checked, there was a bet, a call, the button folded, then the small blind and I called. This was my first mistake. I should not have called a bet with nothing but a draw for half the pot.

The turn brought a 4♠. Now I had the nut low and a straight. I didn't have any reason to think the straight was good. But the low was good. The small blind checked, I bet, they all called. My bet probably wasn't all that smart, if the flop bettor had the nut flush he could have raised here, folding the small blind and costing me money. Also, there was the chance one of the two also had a nut low, in which case I would get only a quarter of the pot. But I didn't get raised, so it seemed to work out even though it probably wasn't real smart. And of course, there was that slim chance my straight was good.

The river was a 2♣. Now my hand was nothing. My A♠ 5♦ made a low, but it was beat by anybody with an A3. The small blind and I checked. There was a bet, a raise, the small blind check raised.

Now my final, and biggest, mistake: I called. I didn't have any of it. It was a terrible call on the river.

When you start making the kinds of mistakes I made on this hand, it's time to cash in, go home, and take a nap.

GENERAL COMMENTS ON THE HI/LO SPLIT GAMES

You'll sometimes hear that hi/lo split games require a different skill set from "regular" poker. This is simply not true. What is different in hi/lo split games is the importance of draws and the lack of importance of big pairs. Putting a lot of emphasis on big pairs isn't a "skill," but it is a habit you need to change if you play hi/lo split games.

BOOKS ON HI/LO SPLIT GAMES

Most general introductions to poker have a short section on Omaha. Some have a section on Omaha hi/lo. But, the treatment in general introductory books is almost always superficial.

A few books have been published that are devoted to hi/lo split games. But none really rate more than just barely adequate. The current books seem to be aimed at the rank beginner with very little poker experience at all and, for the most part, none of them offer any particular insight. This lack of really good books on the game is part of what makes the game so profitable for a good player.

One exception is *The Archer Method: An Expert's Guide to Winning at Poker* by John Archer (1978). He covers seven-card stud hi/lo split and offers considerable insight into this game. The only drawback is that the book was written before the cardroom explosion, so he emphasizes the player-declare version typically played in home games rather than the cards-speak version found in cardrooms. If you can find a copy, it's well worth getting.

The only book I'm aware of that covers the cardroom versions of both seven-card stud hi/lo split and Omaha hi/lo split is *High-Low-Split Poker: Seven-Card Stud and Omaha Eight-or-better for Advanced Players* (1992) by Ray Zee. It's a popular book, but it doesn't really offer all that much. It's aimed at the experienced player who will be playing against tough opponents, but it doesn't really hit its target. Its treatment of Omaha hi/lo split is very basic, and the seven-card stud hi/lo split treatment isn't much better.

There are a number of other books on Omaha hi/lo split, but I don't think any of them are particularly worthwhile.

6

Position

Aggression is everything in poker. But it has to be selective, careful aggression. Blind, constant aggression is just throwing away money. Erratic, maniacal aggression is pointless. The most important factor in the selection of the time and place to show aggression is position. In real estate it's location, in poker it's position. Good position is a primary source of value for many poker hands. It's often more important than the cards themselves are. Aggression is how you realize value, but position and the use of position in guiding your aggression is the source of the value.

Your position determines how much information is available to you when it's time to make a decision. Assuming you can evaluate and use it correctly, the more information you have, the better decision you will make. Also, the less information your opponents have about your hand, the more likely it is they'll make a bad decision. Position controls both sides of this coin: how much information you have and how much information your opponents have.

The value associated with position is easily demonstrated by looking at hold'em or Omaha—games where position remains fixed for each betting round. In these games, if you're in late position, every player (with the exception of the blinds in the first betting round) has to act before you in each betting round. Throughout the play of the hand, you'll have the maximum information about other's hands, while they'll have to act with a minimum level of information about your hand.

If you're holding a hand like A♣ 8♣, it's a lot easier to bet into a field of four players with a flop of K♥ 8♦ 4♣ if they've all checked, than it is if you're first to act. This is not to say you shouldn't be betting this hand from early position, but it is a lot more iffy than it is from late position after everyone has checked.

EARLY POSITION

Position and hand selection are tied together. You really can't make a rational decision about whether or not to play a hand, and how to play it, without first considering your position relative to the first player to act.

This is because of the information you have (or don't have) as a function of your position. Some hands quickly lose value against a raise. Examples that we looked at earlier are Omaha hands like K♠K♥ 2♦ 3♣ or K♠ K♥ A♦ 6♠. When you have such a hand in early position, you should usually fold because the risk of a raise is just too large. But this same hand from late position can become a powerhouse once you've learned that 80 percent of the field didn't raise.

Careful hand selection is important in early position—the first two or three spots after the blinds in hold'em or Omaha and the first couple of players after the bring-in in seven-card stud. It's critical in hold'em. You need to be very careful in early position. In hold'em, you have almost no information about the other players— all you know is your own hand. And at each betting round, you'll have to act first. You'll always have to act before any new information comes available.

In stud, if you're first to act after the bring-in, you only know each player's upcard. This is more information than you have in hold'em when you're first, which is part of the reason position is so much more important in hold'em, but even then, you're at a disadvantage by being first, no matter how many cards you can see.

You have to act based only on the information you have, and since it's limited, you're usually going to be better off if you look for reasons to fold from early position. Rather than looking at your hand to try to determine value, you should be looking at your hand to identify weaknesses, risk factors, or anything less than maximum strength or power. Fold all but the very strong starting hands. This means stick with big cards in hold'em and big cards that are live in stud.

A hand like 6♥ 7♥ in hold'em lacks any high-card strength. K♥ 9♥ has weak high-card strength. A♥ J♦ lacks flush potential. In seven-card stud, a hand like (2♥ 7♥) 6♥ lacks high-card strength, (2♥ 7♥) K♥ has weak high-card strength and what strength it does have comes without any deception value. (A♥ J♦) 10♣ has no flush potential and only a possibility of a high pair. In Omaha hi/lo split, a hand like A♥ 3♣ 9♦ 9♠, with weak prospects for high and weak prospects for low, has no scoop potential of note.

Hands with these kinds of weaknesses usually should be folded from early position. It's often okay to play weak or marginal hands from late position, sometimes even with a raise, but playing them from early position can be suicide.

In Omaha hi/lo hands that don't contain an A2 or AA, they should be folded from early position. And even some of the A2 or AA hands should probably also be folded. In an aggressive game, you should fold an early position A♥ A♦ 9♠ 8♣.

In seven-card stud hands like (K♥ 7♣) 7♦ or (6♥ 7♦) 5♣, they should be folded from early position. Even from late position on the first round, if the player to your immediate right has the high card, you should probably fold weak starts because you'll likely be in early position on fourth street.

Omaha hi/lo split games are often fairly passive preflop. A lot of Omaha hi/lo players don't like to raise before they've seen the flop. Don't let their preflop passivity convince you that it's okay to limp in from early position with weak hands, because you know there probably won't be a raise. You'll still be in early position on the later streets when they do start raising, and a weak start is likely to give you a weak hit on the flop. But it is usually correct to limp from early position with your strong hands. Omaha hi/lo split is a volume game, so you want to be drawing best and getting a good price for drawing. An early position raise usually hurts your price by driving out potentially second-best draws.

HAND TYPES

I've already talked about initial hand selection for the first betting round of the various games. Not all hands are equal. One way to provide a guide to initial hand selection is to think of starting hands as groups of hands of a certain type.

Hand Types and Position in Hold'em

In my previous book, *The Complete Book of Hold'Em Poker* (1999), I categorized starting hold'em hands as dominating hands, power hands, drawing hands, speculative hands, and gambling hands. The categories are shown in table 6.1.

Table 6.1
CARSON HAND GROUPS

Dominating power hands	99 and up, A♣K♣, A♣Q♣, A♣K♦
Dominated power hands	88, A♣9♣, A♣10♣, A♣J♣, K♣10♣, K♣J♣, K♣Q♣, Q♣10♣, Q♣J♣, J♣10♣, A♣Q♦
Drawing hands	77, 66, A♣8♣, K♣9♣, 10♣9♣ A♣J♦K♣Q♦, plus power hands
Speculative hands	55, A♣ 7♣, K♣ 7♣, K♣8♣, Q♣8♣, Q♣9♣, J♣8♣, J♣9♣, 10♣8♣, 9♣8♣, 8♣7♣, 7♣6♣, A♣10♦, K♣J♦, plus drawing hands

Table 6.1 (*cont.*)
CARSON HAND GROUPS

Gambling hands   22, 33, 44, A♣2♣ to A♣6♣, K♣2♣ to K♣6♣, Q♣5♣ to Q♣7♣, J♣7♣, J♣8♣, 10♣7♣,9♣7♣, 8♣5♣ to 8♣7♣, 7♣4♣, 7♣5♣, 6v4♣, 6♣5♣, 3♣5♣, 4♣5♣, A♣9♦, K♣10♦, Q♣10♦, Q♣J♦, J♣10♦

Dominating hands are very strong hands that are likely to dominate the hands being played by others (a hand is dominated if it has three or fewer outs), A♥ K♥ and A♥ Q♥are among the dominating hands.

Though power hands are strong hands, they run the risk of being dominated by strong holdings of others. Power hands should be played judiciously if a tight player shows preflop aggression. An A♥ J♥ or A♥ 9♥ are examples of hands in the power hand group.

Drawing hands are hands that need to get some odds to be effective. A♥ 8♥ is a drawing hand, not quite as strong as an A♥ 9♥, so you should be sure of two or three callers before committing to an A♥ 8♥.

Speculative hands are hands that get their value from having loose callers. A♥ 7♥ is an example of a speculative hand. It's a weak hand and has a flush potential but a very marginal 7 as a kicker to that Ace. This weak 7 needs the odds from getting four or five callers.

Gambling hands are hands that are longshot draws, and they need the odds that correspond to the longshot chances. An A♥ 6♥ or J♥ 8♥ are gambling hands. You shouldn't bother with these hands unless you're sure of six or more callers.

An exception to the suggested odds might be when you have extra blind money in the pot. You can play speculative or gambling holdings at lesser odds when the pot has extra dead money. A third blind (posted by a new player) is at least partially dead money since the hand of the blind player is a random hand and probably very weak.

In early position, you should generally stick with the dominating hands against typical opponents and the power hands against loose opponents. The other hands are too risky from early position when you have essentially no information about how the hand is likely to develop. In later position, after three or four players have acted (folded, called, or raised), you can often play a wider range of hands.

To avoid giving attentive players too much information about your hand, you should sometimes play weaker hands from early position. But you don't want to overdo this. Coming in with a raise with a hand like J♥ 10♥ (in a tight game) or K♥ 10♥ (in a loose game) will serve to keep your opponents guessing about your hand strength.

Hand Types and Position in Seven-Card Stud

You can use the same schema, dominating hands, power hands, drawing hands, and speculative hands to categorize starting hands in seven-card stud. You'll almost never get the kind of odds you'd need to pursue the weak gambling hands in stud, so I omit this category.

Table 6.2
CARSON'S HAND GROUPS FOR SEVEN-CARD STUD

Dominating hands	3 of a kind
	A♥ A♠ x
	K♥ K♠ x♠
	K♥ K♠ Q♦
Power hands	KKx, QQx, JJX, 1010A
Drawing hands	77A, 5♠ 5♠ 6♥, 9♠ 10♠ J♥ two suited,
	A♠ x♠ x♠
Speculative hands	4♠ 5♠ 6♥ two suited, 9♠ 10♥ J♦
	rainbow, 22x

Live cards matter a lot in these categorizations.

LATE POSITION IN HOLD'EM

Information and Late Position

Using Information. The useful information in late position consists of two different categories, both useful when evaluating the value of something like an A♣ 7♣. First of all, you know what kind of odds you're getting. Most of the money to be made with a hand like A♣ 7♣ (or a hand like A♣ 7♣ 8♣ in seven-card stud) comes from flushes and most of the time you won't flop a draw. Most of the time you'll miss the flop completely. So you want good odds from callers. If you're getting good odds, it's worth a raise if you also have that second piece of information: no one else has raised. If you have an Ace with a medium-sized kicker, you're in late position, and no one ahead of you has raised, then the odds are that if you flop an Ace it will be enough to win in all but the most passive of games.

Of course, if someone has raised, you probably don't want to call with A♣7♣. The chances of being dominated by a better Ace is just too great. If there has been a raise and three or four callers, it might be worth cold calling with an A♣ 7♣ though. Not because your chances of not being dominated by a better Ace has improved with the extra callers—the chances have gotten worse, not better—but because the extra money is giving you good enough odds to compensate for this risk. The nature of the risks in hold'em is such that you're almost always being compensated for the extra risks from the money you get from more callers. In most games, you'll frequently have to make a judgment call about a tradeoff between the risk of being dominated and the money odds you're getting. Making that tradeoff gets a lot simpler from late position.

When the game gets loose, concerns about hand domination in hold'em become less important.

Gutshot and Overcard. Many hands benefit from position because of the extra information available. Such hands tend to be marginal at best from early position, but can be very powerful from late position.

A hand I played recently illustrates how position and available information can effect the value of a hand like A♣ J♥. I was on the button. Everyone folded to the player on my right, who limped, I raised with an A♣ J♥, the blinds folded, the limper called.

In most games, an A♣ J♥ isn't worth much from early position. You certainly don't want to have to call a raise from a player behind you and if you open with a raise you won't be real happy if a tight player behind you cold calls. But the hand becomes powerful when played on the button. Now you know what they have before they know anything about what you have. In the previous case, I knew that the player who limped in had a weak drawing hand. The player was a straightforward player, not tricky at all. With any kind of high card or pair strength, even the most passive player would have raised from his position. But he didn't. So I did.

The flop was Q♥ 10♦ 3♣. I had a gutshot straight draw and an overcard. The rainbow flop ensured that any of the four Kings would make me the nuts. Often, the overcard with a gutshot can't be relied on to be good because of the chance that an Ace will make someone a straight. But in this situation, heads up with this flop, spiking the Ace would have probably been good, if Ace high wasn't already good.

When my lone opponent checked the flop, I upped my estimate of the chances both that I already had the best hand, and, if I didn't, that an Ace on the turn or river would be good for me. I bet and he called.

The turn brought an 8♠. My hand just got better by picking up an extra four outs for a straight. Sometimes, I'll grasp any slim improvement as an excuse to bet, which I did as soon as he checked. But he called again.

The river brought a 2♥. I had an Ace high. He checked. I bet again and he folded.

My bet on the river was probably a mistake. He wasn't likely to fold a pair or to call without one. But I thought I might get a call from him with a worse Ace high than mine. Not likely, but maybe. Also, I didn't want to have to showdown my hand and show the table that I'd been betting without a pair. This latter reason was the main reason I bet. Even so, in retrospect I think the bet was a mistake. It's often better to check on the river to entice a bluff than to make a thin value bet.

But a debate about whether I should have bet the river or not isn't really the point here. The point is to consider how differently this hand would have played out if I'd been in early position rather than on the button.

If I'd limped from early position and gotten a caller, I don't know that I would have bet the flop. I probably would have still won the pot, but it would have been a very small pot. And if I checked on the flop and he took the lead and kept betting, I probably wouldn't even have won it.

If I had opened with a raise and had a player cold call, would I like betting that flop as first to act? I might have bet the flop but checked the turn after he called. I don't think he had a pair, so I probably would have won a showdown on the river. But the pot would have been one big bet of his money smaller if I'd checked the turn. Those extra bets you can get from late position add up.

Thin Value Bets from Late Position. Late position can sometimes get you an extra bet into the pot from a thin value bet on the river. A value bet is a bet that (just barely) figures to win if called.

In another hold'em game, I was dealt 2♦ 2♥ in the cutoff position with two players limping in ahead of me. Such a low pocket pair isn't usually worth playing, but the two players who had limped in, plus the players left behind me, were all loose players who tended to chase with very weak hands. If I got lucky and hit a flop, I thought it would pay off. I called, the button called, and both blinds joined us. I got lucky and the six of us saw a flop of J♦ 2♣ 10♥.

It was checked to me and I bet my set. The button folded and I got two callers.

The turn was Q♦. They checked again and both called my bet.

The river brought A♥, and any King would make a straight. But again they both checked. I bet. I got one caller who mucked when I showed my set of twos.

It was my late position that allowed me to make that thin value bet on the river. I got a call from a hand that really couldn't beat anything but a bluff. And that was the only kind of hand I could beat. The same hand, from early position, would not have earned as much. This is why you can sometimes play small pairs from late position but should almost never play them from early position. Marginal hands can be played more aggressively from late position and will make more money when they're good.

Unsuited Big Cards from Late Position in Hold'em

There is an error in David Sklansky and Mason Malmuth's popular hold'em book, *Hold'em Poker for Advanced Players* (1999), that says that two big unsuited cards lose value in loose games. Nothing could be further from the truth. Regardless, this error has created a popular idea that two big unsuited cards shouldn't be played against multiple opponents. Far from it—you should be raising. At least from late position this is what you should be doing. However, the hands should probably be abandoned when one or more opponents have shown strength by raising from early or mid-position.

They do tend to be tougher to play from early position in aggressive games. The danger when a player in front of you raises is domination from either this player or cold callers; it can be very costly to you when an Ace flops and you hold an Ace, Jack against someone else's Ace, Queen. But if he doesn't raise, and you're in late position with something like a K♣ J♥, you're more likely the one doing the dominating, because his lack of a raise suggests he has something more like J♦ 9♣ than A♦ J♣.

Of course, things don't always work out the way you want. Examples of things not working out are pretty easy to come by. I recently had a K♣ J♦ on the button and raised two loose limpers.

They called along with one of the blinds. The flop was an ugly 6♥ 6♣ A♥ and the big blind bet right into the field. Everybody folded, including me.

You shouldn't always automatically fold when the flop misses you like this. Many players habitually use a paired flop as a bluffing opportunity. So you need to be aware of the player doing the betting. But when the indication is that you're beat, you should just give it up. You're there to win the money, not the pots. Hopelessly chasing after pots that you can't win isn't the way to get the money.

If you make it a habit of raising loose limpers whenever you think you have a slight edge, you will be folding on the flop a lot after a preflop raise. Expect a hand like K♣ J♦ to miss the flop over half the time. As long as you get 3-1 or 4-1 on that preflop raise, you'll still end up with a long-run profit even if you have to give up on the flop most of the time. It's important to put that raise in from late position though—you need to be sure they aren't going to show some aggression themselves—and that enough of them will be calling.

Calling a Raise from Late Position

As I've pointed out, a hand you should fold from early position can be worth a raise, or even calling a raise, from late position. An example would be a hand like A♣ 7♣ on the button if four or five players have limped in. With these odds, and with the benefit of late position on subsequent betting rounds, it's probably worth a raise and calling a raise—the odds you're getting with four or five callers offsets the risk of being dominated. But be sure the hand is suited if it's a big, little hand. That extra insurance of even a backdoor flush is worth enough in most games to make up for only having one big card. You usually don't want to be calling raises with hands like A♦ 10♥ or K♣ J♦, even from late position. But if there are enough callers, you're usually safe calling a raise with suited cards. Just be prepared to dump the hand if it misses the flop.

Button Value Raises in Hold'em

Another hand that usually benefits from position is a midsized pocket pair, 6s, 7s, and 8s. This hand can often be played from late position but can get into trouble if played from early position. If the situation is right, it can be played aggressively from late position, whereas unless there is some chance of stealing the blinds' aggression from early position it can backfire. Sometimes, even pocket 6s are worth a raise from late position.

For example, I was recently dealt 6♥ 6♦ on the button in a loose game. There were four loose limpers when it got to me, I raised, they all called along with the big blind. Although marginal for 6s, five to one is pretty good odds for a middle pair. They have a lot of ways to win other than the ideal of flopping a set. And you can often win from late position with hands that wouldn't win from early position. In the loose game, I was in a raise from early position that would almost never win the blinds but that would tend to cut down on the number of callers hurting my odds.

Of course, when the flop was J♣ A♥ K♦ and there was a bet in front of me, the value dried up and blew away. But such value raises don't realize their worth every hand—this is why they require the odds. And even though you can't be sure of getting the odds on your raise unless you're in late position, they are seldom worth playing from early position.

Aces in Hold'em

The effect on hand value of the late position delay in giving your opponents information can be clearly demonstrated by thinking of pocket Aces. Before the flop, you know you have the best hand, so you want to get as much money as possible into the pot. From late position this is easy to do—you just raise after players in front of you have limped in. But from early position it's not so clear: if you raise, you might not get the callers you want, and if you limp, hoping to back-raise, you might not get the raise from another player that you're counting on. AA is so powerful that it qualifies as a disaster if you raise with pocket Aces and just win the blinds.

Position is about information. In late position, the information you have is maximized while the information your opponents have is minimized.

Don't underestimate the strength of pocket Aces, and don't underestimate the power of being last. In the case of a big pair, the value of being last comes from being able to withhold information on the strength of your hand until the last minute.

POSITION IN SEVEN-CARD STUD

Let's say you start out a stud hand with (K♣ K♠) 9♣. This is a pretty good start. But how you'll want to play the hand depends on your position, the upcards of the other players, and the position of the other upcards.

If one of the upcards is an Ace, you should probably raise, but not always. If the Ace is after you, a raise will serve to knock the hand out in most cases, eliminating a potential concern in the later betting rounds. But if you're in early position, right after the bring-in, and the Ace is an aggressive player, you might want to just call the bring-in, intending to reraise after the Ace raises. However, don't count on this raise from anyone other than a very aggressive player.

If your cards are dead, say you have (Q♣ Q♠) 4♥ and a Queen and a 4 are showing in the upcards, you should probably fold in early position but raise the maximum in late position if no one with an overcard to your Queens has played. You're hoping to win it right there with the raise. From early position, there just isn't enough money in the pot to risk it.

Projecting Your Position in Seven-Card Stud

Seven-card stud isn't considered a positional game, because your position is subject to change with every betting round. The high hand goes first, and the high hand might change with every card. But if the high hand consists of a big pair, you can be fairly sure your position won't change on the next card. Of course, having an opponent with an exposed high pair isn't real good news. Regardless, there are some situations where knowing you'll have late position (or early position) the next hand might make the difference between calling or folding.

LATE POSITION IN STUD/8

In hi/lo stud, you generally don't want to draw for a high-only hand and big pairs should just be folded. Exceptions occur when you're in late position, however. An example of such an exception is the following lineup:

(X X)	6♠	bring-in
(X X)	A♠	fold
(X X)	J♥	fold
(X X)	7♦	fold
(X X)	J♣	fold
(Q♥ 8♣)	Q♠	
(X X)	10♣	
(X X)	7♠	

I raised with the Queens. If I'd been first to act after the bring-in, I would have folded. But after four players folded (including the dangerous Ace), it was worth the risk of a raise to try to steal the bring-in. The 10 and 7 behind me folded, and the bring-in called the raise and ended up making a low for half the pot, so things didn't completely work out as planned. But it's still an example of a situation created by position where you might want to play a hand differently than you would in a different position. If the Ace and Jack had been behind me, I probably would have folded, because I didn't want to compete against a low draw and another high, even if I had the best of it for high. When I do draw for high in seven-card stud hi/lo, I want to be the only one drawing for it and position helps me with information about this risk.

POSITION IN OMAHA/8

Position is a critical factor in Omaha hi/lo split. There are many hands that you don't want to raise with from early position because you don't want potentially second-best draws to fold (you want to limp then reraise if someone else raises behind you). These same hands become raising hands from late position. These hands are the solid low draws, hands like A♣ A♠ 2♠ 3♥, A♣ 2♣ 2♠ 3♦, A♠ 2♣ 3♥ 4♦, or similar hands. How you play these types of hands depends entirely on your position.

Some of the strong high-only hands, like A♠ K♦ Q♠ 10♦ also make you more money when you have many second-best draws contributing to the pot, and they should be played similarly to the strong low draws.

At the same time, there are a few hands that have decent prospects, but aren't worth calling a raise with. Some of the big pair hands, hands with a KK in them for example, fall into this category. You might sometimes raise with those hands from late position but fold them from early position because of the risk of a raise from a stronger hand.

The reason you want to fold hands like K♠ K♥ A♦ 6♣ from early position is that you don't want to call raises with the hand. From late position you might want to raise with a hand like K♠ K♥ A♦ 6♦. To illustrate this, I did some equity calculations for K♠ K♥ A♦ 3♣ against various lineups.

Table 6.3
PREFLOP EQUITY FOR K♠ K♥ A♦ 3♣

Hand	Equity %	vs.	Equity %
K♠ K♥ A♦ 3♠	38	A♠ 2♥ 3♦4♣	40
		5♠ A♥ 6♦ 7♣	21
		2♠ 4♥ 6♦ 9♣	18
		Q♠ J♥ 2♦ 3♣	23
K♠ K♥ A♦ 3♣	37	A♠ A♥ 3♦ 4♣	63

Table 6.3 (*cont.*)
PREFLOP EQUITY FOR K♠ K♥ A♦ 3♣

Hand	Equity %	vs.	Equity %
K♠ K♥ A♦ 3♣	34	A♠ 2♥ 3♦ 4♣	29
		2♠ 4♥ 6♦ 9♣	
		2♠ 3♥ Q♦ J♣	

The hand holds its own fairly well unless it's heads up against a strong hand. A raise from another player (presumably with a strong hand) that knocks out other players is a disaster. But against a typical field of three or four opponents, most of them with weak hands, the hand does very well. Fold it from early position, and raise with it from late position against a handful of loose limpers.

POSITION AND THE OTHER PLAYERS

When we talk about position, we usually mean position in reference to the first player to act. But often, position relative to specific players is as important as position relative to the under the gun player. The action is often driven by specific loose and aggressive players rather than the betting order.

Position and Seat Selection

This recommendation is often given to pick a seat where an aggressive player is on your right. This way you'll know whether or not he will raise before you have to act. An exception occurs, however, when the aggressive player is both loose and very aggressive and when the game itself tends to be loose.

At a loose table, you'll often be getting good enough odds to risk having to call a raise with marginal holdings. And if the player is both loose and very aggressive, you don't really gain any extra information by having him act ahead of you, because you know he's likely to raise anyway.

Having the aggressive player on your left lets you get maximum money out of your big hands. You can check, let him bet, then after the field has already called one bet you can raise.

In some situations, the best seat choice is probably to put yourself halfway across the table from the aggressive player. This maximizes your ability to squeeze loose callers for multiple bets in the betting rounds after the flop.

Of course, you don't always get a choice of seat. But you can ask the dealer for a seat change button, which gives you an option to move to the next seat that comes open. You can always decline the option, so getting a seat change button as a matter of course is a good idea.

Position Relative to the Bettor

Usually, when we say position we mean relative to the player who will be first to act. But this is not always the player who will bet first, and sometimes it's your position relative to the player who is the lead bettor that is the important factor.

Playing nine handed, I was fifth to act before the flop with an A♣ 2♣. Two players limped in before me, I raised in the hope of getting the two players behind me to fold, buying myself the button and last position. It didn't work, the button called, but so did both blinds, so I had five callers of my raise, giving me good enough odds on the raise. And four of them would act before me, leaving me with pretty good, but not perfect, position.

My raise was probably marginal at best, but I got lucky and things worked out for me anyway. Sometimes, especially when I've been playing too long, I push some of these marginal hands more than I should. It's a hole in my game I need to plug.

The flop was a very good one for my hand 4♣ 6♥ 3♣—a nut flush draw and a gutshot to a mediocre straight. And, of course, the Ace overcard. If it was checked to me, I intended to bet with this holding. But the first three players checked and the lead bet came from the player to my immediate right. Now I had four players behind me who hadn't called a bet yet. I would have liked to raise, but I didn't want odds on the raise. So I just called, hoping to get as many callers as I could. Everyone called. It was doubtful that they would have all cold called two bets.

I made my flush right away, the turn was the 10♣. Again, the first three players checked and the player on my right bet. Again, I just called, going for the overcalls. But this time the button on my immediate left raised. Two of the early checkers folded, one of them called, the lead bettor called, and I raised. They all called. I didn't want to force players to a decision about cold calling two bets, but most players would automatically call a raise, or even a reraise, once they had put some money in the pot in that betting round.

The turn actually made my nut flush a little better, it was a 5♥, putting a four-card straight on the board. This was good for my hand in that it made it more likely I would get callers from a straight. This time everyone checked to me, I bet, two of them called.

I don't know what they called with, because they didn't show their hands. No matter, the point of this hand is that you often have to adjust your plans based on your position to the lead bettor.

Posting as a New Player

In most rooms, a new player in a game that uses blinds must either post a third blind (the size of the big blind) or wait until it's his turn to post the big blind before he gets a hand. You don't get any free hands without posting a blind first, from whatever position you come in at. If the button has just passed your seat, you should go ahead and post. If you're only two or three hands to the left of the big blind, you should wait for the blind.

In some cardrooms, you are given an option to post the big blind when it gets to you the first time or to wait until the button passes you and post a big blind from late position. When you have this option, you should take it in games that have a structure where the small blind is half or more of the big blind. It's much better to post just the one blind from late position than to post two blinds from early position, even if posting from late position means you don't get dealt a hand on the button.

Position Is Key

Position is the key variable that should be considered at every decision. Your position relative to the button, to the lead bettor, and to the field of callers are all critical pieces of information.

7

Aggression

Aggression is what it's all about. Betting and raising, which put pressure on the other players to make tough decisions, are how you put the other players in a position to make mistakes. And your opponents' mistakes are the source of your money in playing winning poker.

Using aggression at the table is a form of taking control. No one is going to give you control of the table. You have to take it.

Of course, you need to be somewhat selective in your aggression. You need to consider a combination of many factors. In particular, the most important factors are usually your position, cards, and your opponents and how these factors combine in a particular situation.

AGGRESSION AND POSITION

In the previous chapter, I gave some examples of how some hold'em hands that should be folded from early position can become raising hands from late position. One of the reasons for this in hold'em is that you'll still be in late position on later betting rounds. It can be particularly advantageous to be in late position on the flop.

The same situation can arise in seven-card stud—hands that you'd fold from early position but raise in late position. An example is (3♥ A♥) 3♣, where a deuce has the bring-in. Say, for example, an exposed King calls immediately following the bring-in and no Ace is exposed. If you are immediately following the King, you should probably fold, but if you're last, there is a good chance you'll still be last to act on fourth street, so a raise is in order.

Initial hand selection isn't the most critical decision for most hold'em players The most critical decision is made on the flop. In the previous chapter, we saw some examples of situations where the value of late position was mostly realized on the flop bets.

Usually, poker hand value is realized through aggression. This is not to say that there's not a place in the game for calling or folding. In fact, you should probably fold more often than anything else. But when it's time to get the money, you should usually be betting or raising. A bet will win a lot more pots than a call.

Aggression from Late Position

Aggression from late position is aggression that pays off in different ways. If everyone else has checked, indicating weakness,

- A bet can often win the pot, or at least narrow the field, increasing your chance of winning.
- You can make thin value bets.
- They'll often call with as little as one overcard, thinking you're bluffing.

If there has been a bet with multiple callers, you can raise for value with a strong draw.

An Example with Suited Aces in Hold'em. An example of a hand that can pick up value from late position is an Ace suited with a small or medium-ranked card. Something like A♥ 6♥. Weak Aces can often pick up bets after everyone else has checked. You can bet top pair, weak kicker from late position with more confidence than you can from up front, and you can often semibluff raise with a draw.

Being suited tends to mute the risk of domination, where domination is defined as having three or fewer outs. Ace, Queen offsuit is dominated by Ace, King, for example. It has to catch a Queen to catch up. But a suited Ace, Queen isn't dominated because of the little bit of extra outs it accrues by being suited. It has outs other than the Queen. Of course, even if suited, an Ace, Queen matched up against an Ace, King is still taking much the worst of it.

Hands like A♥ 6♣ are potentially dominated by many hands, such as 7♠ 7♣, A♣ 8♥. But if this A♥ 6♣ is A♥ 6♥ (suited), it is often worth playing from later position. Adding a flush draw makes many flops stronger. There's really a big difference between flopping second pair and flopping second pair with a backdoor flush draw. Many players don't realize how important that little extra bit is.

He Should Have Bet the Flop. A corollary to the "good things happen to those who bet" rule is that "bad things happen to those who don't bet." I recently played a hand where if a player had bet his bottom pair on the flop, I probably would not have ended up winning the pot.

He was on the button, I was in middle position. Two players limped before me, I raised with an A♥ K♣, one player cold called, our antihero cold called with K♠ 2♠ on the button, both blinds folded, and the two limpers called. Cold calling a raise with that hand was his first mistake.

The flop was J♥ 2♣ 4♦. Everyone checked. I didn't think much of my overcards against four players. Of course, I couldn't be sure, but I thought I would have folded if the antihero would have bet his bottom pair and overcard after everyone checked to him. I usually don't call with just two overcards in a loose game with many active hands seeing the flop. There was actually a good chance his bottom pair was good after everyone checked. But he didn't bet and the turn brought us K♦.

Now I bet, and I wasn't going anywhere. Curiously, he didn't raise, he just called with his two pair, along with one other player. Of course, I wouldn't be the hero if A♦ hadn't come on the river, my top two pair beating his two pair.

Of course, he probably shouldn't have called the raise preflop to begin with, but if he was going to play with a deuce, then he should have bet it if it paired and it looked like the flop didn't hit anybody else. A bet on the flop from him probably would have won him that pot.

I Should Have Fired Twice. When you think you have the best hand, you should keep betting. Failure to bet is giving the other players a free card, a card that might well beat you.

I made the mistake of checking the turn with a pocket pair of 8s recently. I was on the button and was dealt 8♠ 8♣. Three players limped in and I raised, the blinds folded, and the limpers called.

I like to raise with midsized pairs from the button when any number of players have limped. It's likely anyone with a higher pair would have raised before me and my raise helps take control of the betting. I'm likely to give it up if too many overcards flop, but if the opponents are a little passive, they aren't likely to bet into me on the flop after a raise unless they can beat me. So the raise preflop helps me save some bets those times overcards do flop and I'm beat.

2♦ 2♣ J♥ was the flop. They all checked.

These players were all somewhat passive and fairly straight-forward. They would probably bet right out with a deuce. With a Jack, they might check with a weak kicker, but they would probably bet a Jack. So I thought I had the best hand. I bet. When two of them folded and one called, it seemed very likely I was the best. The caller was a very loose player who tended to call with almost anything.

The turn was a 7♦. At this point, my brain seemed to have sputtered and ran out of gas. I thought I was best on the flop. Nothing had happened that caused me to change that assessment. My opponent checked the turn. Then I checked. I didn't bet. I should have bet. I had no reason not to think I had the best hand. But even on the best of days it seems that there will be instances where my brain just misfires, doesn't work right one time. This was one of those times.

It turns out that he had K♥ 4♥. He called on the flop hoping to either catch a King or pick up a flush draw. When neither came on the turn, I'm pretty sure he would have folded to a bet on the turn. But I didn't bet.

The river was K♦. At least he mercifully didn't bet on the river.

Aggression from Early Position

Usually, being first isn't the best situation to be in. Having to act first, before anyone else has had to do anything to give you a clue about their holdings, can be a handicap. Against a large field of opponents, it's almost always a handicap.

Sometimes being first is an asset though. When you're heads up against a weak player, you can often just bet without any regard at all to your hand and win it. But this is not the situation you'll find yourself in most of the time.

Most of your early position bets will probably come from big blind hands in unraised pots. This means the pot will be relatively small and your hand will be relatively weak Often, the best thing to do in this situation is just give it up. Check and fold to a bet. But at times you'll pick up something on the flop, and an unraised pot means a small pot, but it also means they don't have much. Against weak opposition you can often just bet and take it. It's important to know the tendencies of your opponents in big blind situations. There isn't a one size fits all answer. Your overall tendency should be to give up easily when the pot is small and compete for it aggressively when it's large.

Avoiding Free Cards. You don't want to give your opponents a free chance to beat you. Let's say you have J♠ J♦ and the flop is 9♥ 7♥ 3♣. You probably have the best hand and there are some important reasons to bet here. What if your opponent has two hearts? Or 10♦ 9♦? Or A♣ 7♣ or 6♣ 8♣? A player with any of these holdings has a chance to beat you. Make him pay to try. If you bet, he is probably getting the correct odds to call, but if you don't bet, you're giving him infinite odds. You can't give away gifts like this very often and expect to be a winning poker player.

Note, however, that we're talking about a single opponent. When you have four or five opponents who call, you may not have such a good hand. The perspective you need to take when evaluating a hand on the flop is different when you have multiple opponents than when you have a single opponent. Against many opponents, you'd still want to bet the hand above, but if someone else bets first, and other players have called, you might be unsure enough about the situation to forego a reraise.

Betting to keep from giving up a free card can be even more important when you're not sure you have the best hand. For example, let's say you're on the big blind with a hand like K♥ 4♦ and no one raised before the flop. The flop is J♣ 4♥ 3♦. What should you do?

You should probably bet. You might not have the best hand. Someone may have a Jack, but the danger of this is not nearly as large as the danger of giving someone with a hand like 10♠ 8♠ or 7♠ 6♠ a free chance to beat you. If someone does have a Jack, you have outs. If you do have the best hand and check, then a lot of cards could come on the turn that will give someone a better pair than your measly pair of 4s. Also, by betting you might get someone with a better hand, like 8♥ 8♦, to fold. The free card concept is often a much more important concept in deciding whether or not to bet than is whether or not you have the best hand.

Pocket 8s under the Gun. As I mentioned, medium-sized pocket pairs in hold'em don't need to flop a set to win or to be worth continuing after the flop. A hand I recently played is an example of raising with 88 and of a board that didn't involve a set or an overpair, but still had a good flop for pocket 8s.

It was a loose, fairly passive game. There were six players who were seeing the flop, but with small pots—there was not much action after the flop. I had two black 8s under the gun and I opened with a raise (the pots I'm involved in tend to be larger than the ones I'm not involved in). All folded to the button who called, the small blind folded, and the player on the big blind called.

I had bad position, but that's why I open raised, hoping to drop everyone but the blinds. It would have been all right to limp with the hand in the loose game, but I chose not to.

Three of us saw the flop of J♥ 7♣ 9♣. A pair and a gutshot. And if I spiked an 8, it could have made somebody a straight, but couldn't have made somebody a flush (because I had 8♣). The player on the big blind checked, I bet, and they both called. It was important to bet. A lot of turn cards could hurt me and I didn't want to give them free odds to draw against me if I was the best at that point. After everyone called, and no one raised, I thought I was the best.

The turn card was a 6♦. That was a good card for me, because it gave me at least three more outs just in case I needed them and it wasn't likely to have improved anyone to a better hand than mine. The big blind checked. I bet. The player behind me folded, and the player on the big blind called.

The river was a Q♣. I didn't like that card so much. The big blind checked. I checked and showed down. I won. I don't know what he had. If I'd have had that hand in late position, I could have bet it on the river and maybe gotten a call from a smaller pair.

This is just an example of a flop for 88, which isn't a great flop, but against just a couple of callers it is well worth pushing on.

The problem with this hand is, of course, the position. Getting hands like this in early position can be a problem in loose games. If the games are very loose, and you know you'll get a lot of callers, then you should probably just limp with the medium-sized pairs, maximizing the odds you get. But in a more typical loose game, where you might get anywhere from about three to six callers, it's probably a good idea to raise early and try to get the number of callers down to two or three.

You can't have the button every time.

When analyzing medium pairs, many people work under a fallacy that you have to flop a set or an overpair to have any value. This hand is an example of a hand that is worth playing aggressively past the flop but isn't a flopped set or overpair. From late position, you should almost always raise loose limpers and probably raise what I'd call typical limpers. Tight limpers are a different story. And early position is a different thing. One of the reasons that you should almost always raise loose limpers is that you'll get enough flops like the one I got so that you don't have to flop a set to lead the betting to the river.

Gutshot to the Nuts but no Overcard. Sometimes you don't know the benefit from a bet until after you've made the bet. So many good things can result from a bet that you can't predict which good outcome you'll get this time. A recent hand I played is an example of a player who didn't follow through on his positional advantage, allowing me to pick up the pot with a bet.

I was in the big blind with an 8♦ 9♥ and got a free ride after two early position limpers and a call from the small blind. The flop was 6♥ 2♦ 10♣. That's not a flop that's likely to have hit anyone and I did have a gutshot. If no one had a 10, I could have even paired and won. That flop screamed for a bet and I gave it one. It was a near perfect semibluff situation.

The bet had some chance of winning, and even though it wasn't likely to catch all three of my opponents with a fold, it could easily have set me up for a winning bet on the turn or river. Plus, I had backup outs just in case I needed them. A lot of players wouldn't bet. I didn't have a made hand and didn't really think I had the best hand. But I didn't completely miss that flop and it was possible that they did. Failure to bet at that point was just giving up prematurely.

The bet seemed to go wrong when the under the gun player raised, and the other two opponents folded. I called the raise but was ready to discount the idea that I could pair and win. Things didn't turn out the way I had hoped, but I think the bet was still the right thing to do, that the bet worked out well often enough to make it right.

The turn was a 3♣. I checked, ready to fold, but he checked behind me. We had both been semibluffing on the flop. The difference was I now knew he was raising on a draw (probably just overcards) but he didn't know I didn't have a pair of 6s or some such hand.

So when a 6♣ came on the river, I bet right out, confident that the pot was mine unless he was willing to call with a no-pair, high card. As I expected, he folded. The other player had better position than I did on that hand. But he didn't fully utilize his position. He had an advantage but he let it pass. A bet by him on the turn, after I showed weakness with my check, would have won the pot for him. My flop bet was probably the reason for his failure to follow through on the turn. His flop raise had just been an attempt to get a free card on the turn—he had no clue that he had the best hand. Good things happen to those who bet.

Second Pair. In loose, passive games, second pair is a hand that should usually be bet from early position, but folded from late position if someone else has bet.

The reason you should fold from late position if someone else has bet is that passive players seldom bet less than top pair from early or midposition and you're drawing to only five outs. In a raised pot, where the pot odds are larger, it might be worth taking a card off. In a more aggressive game, where players are likely to bet a wider range of hands, second pair isn't an automatic fold, it might be the best hand.

The reason you should bet from early position is that loose players will call with a lot of hands that can't beat second pair but they won't bet those hands. They'll call with overcards, three-card straights, or a King, Queen if the board has an Ace—a very wide range of hands. Sure, sometimes you'll bet and won't have the best hand, but getting two or three callers who have only a glimmer of a hope of beating a second pair occurs often enough to make up for it.

Another reason that betting second pair into a field of loose, passive players is a good idea is that they'll not only call with worse hands, they often won't raise with better hands. A hand I recently played illustrates some of the benefits of playing against passive players.

I was on the big blind with 7♦ 6♥. Playing five handed, two players limped, the small blind called, and I checked. The flop was 2♦ K♦ 7♣. The small blind checked, I bet, and all three called. They didn't all have flush draws, so now it was a pretty good chance one of them had a King or a better 7, so I wasn't real happy about the developments. But the turn made things a lot better, 7♥.

The small blind checked again, and I bet again. This time, two players folded and I only got one caller. The turn was a 2♣, I bet, he raised, and I reraised. He flopped two pair (K2) and slowplayed it. Passive players often do that—wait until they are beat before they raise. I got lucky, which was the only way I would have won that pot. But if I hadn't gotten lucky, my passive opponent wouldn't have won the maximum number of chips he could have.

Gutshot and Second Pair. I was playing at a low-limit, loose, passive table. On the big blind with Q♥ 9♣, I got a free ride along with three limpers and the small blind. The flop was J♠ 9♦ 8♥.

I had a second pair, a gutshot, and an overcard. Hitting the overcard probably wouldn't be good, but hitting the gutshot probably would be, and the second pair might already be the best hand. The small blind checked, I bet and lost one player.

9♣ came on the turn. I bet and lost one more. 4♣ came on the river. I bet. Both the remaining players folded.

There was nothing spectacular about this hand. I didn't have a particularly strong hand and nothing unusual happened. But I built up the pot with routine aggression. I had a good, solid hand. But it was far from the nuts, and there where many hands that could beat it. Most of the time, there aren't any monsters under the bed, but if you aren't betting your routine hands then you're leaving money on the table.

A check on the river probably would have been even better, to entice a bluff. The one time that passive play is often more profitable than direct aggression is on the river, when it's likely they won't call with a worse hand than yours but they might bluff at the pot if given a chance.

Bet and Take It. Sometimes, you should just bet the flop because you're pretty sure it missed the other guy. For example, let's say you're in the big blind with a couple of random cards and a late position player limps in. Heads up, you see a flop like A♦ J♣ 4♥. This flop may have missed you completely, but it also probably missed the limper. He's not likely to have limped with big cards, because he'd have raised from late position. And he probably would have folded small cards. So his most likely hand is a couple of midsized cards, something like 8♥ 7♣. Bet right out and you'll probably win it. In the same situation, if the flop is something like 9♣ 8♣ 4♦, then you'd need to be a little more careful.

Semibluff from Early Position. A semibluff is a bluff with outs. It's a bet, made when there are cards still to come, that might win right then, but if someone calls there are still cards to come, so it has a chance to improve to the best hand.

Semibluff is a tool of aggression that most players don't use enough. An example of a good situation for a semibluff came up on a hand I played recently.

I had 8♥ 7♣ on the small blind, one player had limped in from the button, I called, the big blind checked, and the flop was 6♥ A♦ 10♣. This was a perfect opportunity for a semibluff:

- There was no raise preflop, which suggested that no one had an Ace.
- It was a rainbow flop, so no one was likely to call with a draw.
- If someone called, I still had the gutshot draw to fall back on.

In this case, I bet and they both folded.

Betting Draws

When to raise with a draw can get complicated to evaluate exactly. You compare the pot odds to the chances that the raise will win you the pot (not the chances of winning the pot). You compare the odds on expected calls (not pot odds) to the chances of improving and winning. There are also chances that your raise won't win the pot for you but increase your chances of winning by knocking out a competing draw. There's lots of potential benefits to a raise, you just need to look at all of them and add them all up.

AGGRESSION AND YOUR CARDS

Some players think of aggressive betting as a way to "protect your hand," a bet they won't call so they can't catch a card that can beat you. Players who think this way will often end up playing passively because "they won't fold anyway." This is not a good way to think about things.

When you bet with the best hand, sometimes you prefer that they fold, but sometimes you do better if they call. When you're betting with the best hand, what you prefer they do depends on the combination of the size of the pot and their chances for improvement to a better hand. It depends more on their hand than on your hand.

Free Cards and Aggression

From early position, you should often use aggression to avoid giving a free card on the flop or turn. You do that by betting whenever there's a pretty good chance you have the best hand.

From late position, you can often use aggression on the flop to get yourself a free card on the turn. You do that by betting or raising from late position when there's a pretty good chance you don't have the best hand but do have a draw to the best hand. The result of this aggression is that they will often check to you on the turn, letting you check and getting two cards for the price of one.

Thin Value Bets

A thin value bet is a bet on the river that figures to win but is a weak hand that only figures to win from a call by a very weak hand.

Some of the low-limit games online have players who will call with as little as King for high, making thin value bets almost mandatory in these games.

The opportunity for thin value bets seems to occur frequently in loose Omaha hi/lo split games. I got a free look at the flop in a recent game with a K♣ Q♠ 6♥ 4♣.

The flop was 5♠ 3♦ J♠, giving me a straight draw for half the pot. I didn't expect to scoop by making a 64 low. It was very unlikely the best low. Calling a bet on a draw for half the pot is generally not a good idea, particularly in a small, unraised pot. The hope that a 6 4 would be good enough for the low half was pretty much just a very faint hope. I should not have called a bet on this flop, but I did. I saw the turn of K♦ with two other players.

Now I still had the straight draw for half the pot and a measly pair. Again, I should not have called a bet, particularly a double-sized turn bet. I'll have to admit, my mind was someplace else during most of this hand. But don't worry, I salvaged it a short while later.

The river was Q♥. Top two pair on the river isn't much of a hand in Omaha. But these two guys were likely to have been chasing a low, so I bet. I got one caller, he showed 4♦ 9♠ K♠ 6♣. Like me, he had a draw for half the pot, but also had a flush draw, so his draw was much stronger than mine, and he had a draw for the whole pot. He called me on the river with nothing but one pair.

His flush draw was for the whole pot because he could make a flush without putting a possible low on the board. I couldn't make my straight draw without putting out a possible low.

My bet on the river was a value bet, but it was a thin one. My thinking was that the flop had a lot of potential draws, none of which got there, one player had been checking and calling, the player who was betting frequently pushed draws, and, finally, I thought he'd make a weak call because my hand looked like a draw that had missed since I'd been check/calling.

Through most of the hand, my play was atrocious—passively calling with only faint hopes of winning anything. But just ignore that and think about the river bet. It was a thin bet. But it was a value bet and it was a good one.

PASSIVE PLAY

Bad Things Happen When You Slowplay

Most players slowplay too much, and it can cost them dearly at times. A slowplay is just a deceptive play where you play a strong hand weakly. The idea is to allow someone else to get a cheap draw to a second-best hand. But there are many ways a slowplay can go wrong.

One way a slowplay can go wrong is for your opponent to have a strong but second-best hand and is slowplaying himself. This situation can cost you a lot of missed bets.

Slowplay Cost Him a Bet

A lot of players get cute with a very strong hand, and rather than getting an extra bet, the cuteness ends up costing them a bet, but they don't realize it.

In a recent nine-handed online game, I was dealt J♥ 5♥ in the cutoff seat.

I made a loose call after one early position limper and the big blind checked. Three of us saw a flop of A♣ J♦ 9♥. Check, check. I bet my second pair, and the big blind called. The 5♣ on the turn gave me two pair. It was checked to me and I bet. He called. The river brought the 8♦ and the big blind check-raised.

The big blind had JJ, didn't raise preflop, flopped a set, and continued his slowplay. I would have raised on the turn if he'd have just straightforwardly bet the flop and turn.

I would have called his flop bet because most players don't limp from early position with an Ace in their hand.

A No-Limit Hand

Another way slowplay can cost you money is when your hand isn't really as good as you think, and a free card can give someone a better hand, not a second-best hand. This is, of course, the worst possible outcome from a slowplay, costing you not just extra bets but the entire pot. The idea of a slowplay is to let them catch up a little bit, not to run right past you.

Sometimes, it can cost you both extra bets and the pot at the same time. An example of this occurred recently when I was playing in a small, no-limit hold'em game.

I made a small raise with A♥ 7♥ and got a call from one of the blinds and the limper. The two other players were ahead of me and they both checked on the flop of 6♥ 5♠ 10♦ and I took the free card. They checked again on the turn. Now, on the turn, the board was 6♥ 5♠ 10♦ 3♠.

I managed to pick up a gutshot straight draw and I had the ace overcard. It wasn't much of a hand, but everyone else had already checked twice. Until then, I wasn't all that interested in the pot. At this point, I thought it was possibly the best hand. I became convinced of that when they both checked again.

I made a bet of about $30 into a $28 pot (the $28 was from pre-flop betting). Both my opponents called. That was surprising to me, and a little unsettling. I was actually sorry I'd bet. Until the river came, that is. A 4 fell, giving me a straight. Again, they both checked and went bust when both called my very large bet.

What did those two players have? One had flopped a top pair, a King and a 10. The other had pocket 5s, flopping a set. The pocket 5s made terrible mistakes in this hand. He slowplayed on the flop when another player was also slowplaying the second-best hand. Then he slowplayed again on the turn when I'd picked up a weak draw to beat him. If he'd made any kind of bet on either of those betting rounds, I would have folded and he would have gotten a call from the player with the top pair. His slowplay cost him a large pot.

A Set of Aces in Another No-Limit Game

There are times when a slowplay is the right thing. But not as many times as most players seem to think. If you've got any doubt whether slowplay is the right move, you probably should just bet.

The idea of slowplay is to give your opponents a chance to catch up a little when you have a very strong hand. But often, your hand isn't as strong as you think and they don't catch up, they zoom right past you.

In a small, no-limit game I play in some Friday nights, I made a bad call that probably could have been avoided if I hadn't slow-played a set of Aces.

It was a hold'em, 50 cent and dollar blinds, no-limit, $20 buy-in game. The game got a little bigger than those nominal figures as the night progressed. When this hand happened, I had about $300, we were six handed, and the money was pretty deep all around the table. Stack sizes ranged from about $100 to about $400.

Two other players were involved in the hand: Matt and Doug. I've played with them both before. They are both very aggressive players, but Doug tends to be pretty tight and plays somewhat straightforwardly, while Matt tends to be pretty loose, and tricky. When Matt's betting, you sometimes just have to call with hands you don't really like calling with. When Doug is betting, you usually want to give it a second thought before calling.

Anyway, I got A♦ A♣ on the big blind, Matt was on the small blind, and Doug was in late position.

Someone from early position limped, Doug limped, Matt limped, I made it $6, opener folded, and Doug and Matt called.

The flop was A♥ 5♦ 8♥.

Matt bet $10.

Ordinarily, I don't like to slowplay sets. But I had Matt betting into me and Doug behind me. Doug knew Matt could be betting anything and knew that I tend to call Matt with a very wide range of hands. If I just called, I thought there was a good chance Doug would raise. So I called. Doug called.

The turn was 4♦.

Matt bet $25, again I just called, and Doug went all in, raising another $140.

I called. I think it was a bad call. I thought about it a long time before I finally did call. It was my slowplay that put me in a bad situation where I had to make a tough decision. It was a crying call, I pretty much thought that I was beat, although I expected to see a 67 instead of the 23 he showed me when a 3♦ came on the river.

I think I made a mistake by not raising on the flop, and an even worse mistake by calling on the turn. Because of the slowplay, he could have been betting a wider range of hands than if I had been aggressive throughout. I hadn't shown any activity that indicated I particularly liked that flop.

By the way, if you think a tight player wouldn't have seen the flop with a 2♣ 3♣, this was a short-handed game with a lot of action. Matt and I are both action players. That night two other players who are usually a little tight by game standards were losing and playing with their noses open a little.

RESPONDING TO AGGRESSION

When playing in an aggressive game, sometimes you have to just suck it up and tough it out. For example, I was playing in a very aggressive online game when I was dealt 7♣ 8♣ on the big blind. Five of us took the flop for two bets. The flop was K♣ Q♣ 9♥. I was first to act and checked my flush draw. There was a bet, a fold, a raise, and a cold call. Then I check-raised. The raiser capped it and the player who cold called folded to the two more bets. Three of us took the turn.

As a side note here, my flop raise was somewhat marginal. I thought I could be sure of getting three callers on the raise, but it turns out I only got two—at best a break-even proposition on the raise.

Anyway, the turn was 9♣, making my flush. I bet it. There was a raise, then another raise. At the time, I just didn't see how my flush could be any good. I folded.

Some blank came on the river, the pot was won by three 9s. The player who had three bet on the turn had top two pair.

This was a very aggressive game. I should have toughed it out with my flush. In a tighter or more passive game, those raises on the turn were a sure indication that my little flush was no good. But in the game I was in, hyperaggression was the norm. I should have factored that into my thinking before I mucked my hand.

Calling a Raise

It's one thing to raise. It's something else entirely to call a raise.

When you raise, you give yourself an extra way to win—everyone may fold. But if you call a raise, the only way you can win is by having the best hand. There are times when you should raise with a hand if no one else has raised, but if someone has already raised you should fold. An example is A♣ 7♣ from late position in hold'em.

8

Outs and Draws

When all the betting is over, we have a showdown. Those with live hands turn them over and the best hand wins the pot. The determination of which hand is best is just a straightforward comparison. A flush beats a straight, two pair beats one pair, a pair of Kings beats a pair of Jacks, and so on. Before all the cards are out, however, the determination of which hand is best isn't quite so straightforward.

When playing razz (seven-card loball), if one player has (A2)34K on fifth street and another has (97)654, who has the best hand? It's not the 9, it's the King. A 9 low beats a King for low, but the King has two chances to catch either a 9, 8, 7, 6, or 5. That's sixteen cards out of forty-two unseen cards and he has two shots at it—while the 9 low has slim redraw possibilities. You don't have to have the best hand to have the best hand. Draws are sometimes a favorite over a made hand.

An example from hold'em is K♥ Q♥ versus A♦ J♦ with a flop of J♥ 10♥ 2♦. The pair of jacks isn't really the best hand—the straight flush draw will win two-thirds of the time.

Draws are more important in some forms of poker than others. Draws are very important in razz and Omaha, for example, but not that important in draw poker (in spite of its name). Draws are often very strong holdings in hi/lo split games and powerful in loose hold'em games.

128

Seemingly small structural changes can materially change the value of a draw. For example, adding a bug (a Joker that acts as a fifth Ace and as a wild card to complete a straight or a flush) to draw poker creates the possibility of a powerful draw such as A♥ K♥ Q♠ Joker, where twenty-four cards make Aces up or better. Doubling the bet size on the river in seven-card stud or hold'em (1-5, 10 on the river stud, or 3/3/6/12 hold'em, as examples) can significantly increase the value of a draw.

MULTIWAY HANDS IN HOLD'EM

Multiway hands are hands that have multiple ways to win—large suited connectors in hold'em are the prime example of a multiway preflop hand. A♠ K♠ can win by making a big pair, a big straight, or a big flush. Many ways to win, and it might even win unimproved.

The Best Draw

It's important not to underestimate the value of a strong draw. I recently played in a short-handed game where I was the aggressor the whole way, and until the river the other guy had both the best hand and a good draw. He just didn't know it.

It was a four-handed game, and I was dealt K♥ 10♥ on the small blind. Two limpers, I raised, and everyone called.

I liked the flop. 8♠ J♠ Q♥. I'd have preferred the two spades not be on the board, but I did have the backdoor flush draw to go with my straight draw with an overcard. I bet and got two callers.

The turn didn't help me at all—4♦. But I still liked my straight draw. I bet, intending to continue the bluff on the river if I lost one more player on the turn. But I didn't lose anybody, they both called.

It turned out that I didn't need to lose anybody though, because the A♣ on the river completed my straight. The Ace had paired the A♥ 10♣ of one of my callers and he called my river bet.

My aggression was probably going to win the pot for me

whether I made my draw or not. Making the draw and having the same card pair him, however, did win me an extra bet on the river.

Even if my opponent had a pair the whole way, I had eleven cards that could beat a pair (if he'd had a pair, he wouldn't have had the straight draw).

When playing hands that you expect to be drawing, it's important that the draw be solid. Marginal starts lead to marginal draws.

Another Strongest Draw

In my previous book, I devoted an entire chapter to the play of one particular hand that resulted in a strong draw on the flop with multiway action. I'm not going to analyze the hand that deeply here, but I'm going to discuss the drawing aspects of that hand.

We have 9♠ 7♠ on the button and five players have limped in ahead of us. We call, the small blind folds, and the big blind raises. Everyone calls.

Seven players are in for a flop of 8♠ 7♥ 4♠. This is a very good flop for us. We have second pair, a flush draw, an overcard, and a backdoor straight draw. We might have the best hand, and if we don't have that, then we have a lot of outs. Counting any 9, a 7, and a spade as an out, we have fourteen outs plus the backdoor straight. Fourteen outs on the flop is about even money to hit at least one of them by the river. We're in very good shape here.

The way the hand plays out, there is a bet and a raise in front of us, and our hero who actually played the hand just calls, then just calls again when the big blind reraises. We should be raising, not calling. We have a powerful, powerful draw and should be getting the money in. Afterward, the player who played this hand explained that he didn't raise because he was afraid someone had a bigger flush draw than him. If you're really that concerned about a bigger flush draw, you should fold this on the flop, but there's no reason for this concern. Even if someone does have a bigger flush draw, you still have other outs.

The turn made the flush with K♠, and a 9♦ came on the river. No one else had a flush.

Pocket Pairs

One thing that's been neglected in the poker literature is the multiway properties of middle-sized pocket pairs. The popular belief is that pocket pairs should be played for the chances of flopping a set.

I simulated a fairly tight hold'em game, raising from under the gun with pocket pairs. Table 8.1 summarizes the results.

The small pocket pairs are net losers when played with aggression, but pocket 8s and up show a meaningful profit from almost indiscriminate aggression. Those middle pairs can be strong hands if played with some discretion.

Table 8.1
POCKET PAIR PERFORMANCE

Pocket Pair	Win (%)	$ Win/Hand
22	30.2	- 4.03
33	31.3	- 3.32
44	32.8	- 2.69
55	34.4	- 1.69
66	36.4	- 0.36
77	44.0	0.07
88	47.2	2.78
99	50.4	5.43
10 10	55.2	10.34
JJ	59.8	15.97
QQ	65.4	23.65
KK	71.2	33.72
AA	82.0	50.34

(The dollars are in a 10/20 game with 5/10 blinds)

Pocket 7s. An example of a midsized pocket pair hitting the flop hard without flopping a set occurred in a recent hand.

I was dealt a pair of 7s on the cutoff seat (one before the button). A loose player limped from a middle position, I raised, the button cold called, the small blind called, and the big blind folded.

The flop was a beautiful 5♥ 3♣ 6♦. With my 7♦ 7♥, I was feeling pretty good, an overpair and a gutshot straight draw and no one had a flush draw. There was a good chance I had the best hand, and if I didn't, I had outs. It was checked to me, I bet, the only caller was the button, the players in front of me folded. I was feeling even more confident now.

The turn paired the board, 3♥. I still thought I was best, I bet. The button raised. I didn't think he had a 3 because he wasn't likely to have cold called two bets before the flop with a 3. But he might have with a 55, 66, or 88. Would he have slowplayed those hands on the flop? Probably yes with the 55 or 66. I think I should have been more aggressive and reraised him here, but I didn't, I just called.

The river was the gutshot 4♣. I checked. Why? The only hands I could beat that I thought he might have was a bluff or a pocket pair of 8s or 9s. If I bet, I expected him to either raise or fold. So the check was giving him a chance to bluff again if that was what he was doing. It turns out he was bluffing, but he just checked and showed down his K♣ Q♦, conceding me the pot. My check on the river didn't work, but was the right thing to do.

The point of this hand is, of course, to show the multiway property of the midsized pairs.

Pushing a Pair of 8s. In another game, I was in early midposition, third to act, and got dealt two black 8s. The two players ahead of me folded and I raised. Raising with 88 was a little bit on the aggressive side in this situation.

Everyone folded to the big blind who called the raise.

I like playing midsized pocket pairs against one opponent. From the number of examples I have in this book, I guess you might conclude that I like playing midsized pairs period. I do prefer, however, that my opponents to be in front of me. This is part of the reason for the raise: to discourage those behind me from calling.

The flop was 3♠ 10♣ 5♦ and he checked I wasn't particularly concerned about the one overcard to my pair. I bet, he called. The turn added the 2♦ to the mix. He bet.

Whoa. What's this? I called. Later, when I discussed this hand on the internet, I was criticized for not having raised here. "What were you afraid of, a 4-6?" I was asked. Well, yes, I was a little worried about that possibility. It also could have been a semibluff with a newly acquired flush draw. He could have had a 10 with a weak kicker and changed his mind and bet. He could have had pocket 3s and initially intended to check raise the turn but got scared I wouldn't bet. He could have had a lot of hands. Some of the hands he could have beat me, and some could have been bluffs. I like my call.

I don't know if he's a bad or good player—I'm not even sure I know what this means. But hands he could have? Any two diamonds. A 10 with a weak kicker. Pocket 3s, 5s, or 4s. An overpair to the 10, A♠, and 4♠. Any of these hands are possible. With some of these hands, many players will check call the flop, intending to check raise the turn, then get scared I won't bet the turn and bet out, foregoing the planned check-raise. I see it often in low-limit games. Some players will check call with a mediocre top pair, worried about overcards, then bet the turn when no overcard falls. A 10♠ 9♣, for example, in this case.

I was probably ahead. But I wasn't sure. If I wasn't ahead, then I had two outs. If I was ahead, then just calling increased the chances he'd bluff a busted flush draw on the river. I thought he was probably betting a flush draw. If that was what he had, then I needed to raise. But he could have had a wide range of hands where a raise would not have been real smart. However, a raise might have been okay. Of course, folding wasn't a good idea.

The river brought a 7♣.

He checked. I bet. He called and showed pocket 4s.

In hindsight, his bet on the turn was a semibluff, he'd picked up a straight draw. I still think my call was right though. If I'd raised the turn, I don't think he would have called a bet on the river. I basically played my hand like A♠ K♣.

Pairs Don't Always Work Out. Of course, middle pairs don't always work out, even when they seem to hit the flop well. In a recent hand, I was dealt pocket 5s on the button, raised when everyone folded to me, and one of the blinds called. I liked the flop of 4♥ 6♦ 6♥. My single opponent checked, I bet he called.

I didn't like the turn of Q♥ as much as I'd liked the flop. But when he checked again, I bet again. And he called again.

Even after the river card of 4♣, I still thought the chances were good that I was best. Until he bet out that is. I folded.

I thought it was very, very unlikely he was bluffing when he bet out. He'd already passed two opportunities to bet scare cards. So I was confident that I was beat when he finally bet the river. He did show his hand: K♠ Q♣

MULTIWAY HANDS IN OMAHA/8

Draw That Missed

When thinking about draws, you want to start with a hand that gives you as strong of a chance as you can get—generally hands with multiple possibilities.

Omaha hi/lo split is such a game, where you pretty much only want to play hands that have strong draw possibilities: Broadway cards, wheel cards, and suited Aces. An example of a hand that doesn't fall into this category is 3♥ Q♥ 2♦ J♦. It has plenty of potential for second-best flush, second-best straights, or second-best low. I was recently dealt this hand on the small blind and I took a look at the flop for half a bet. Five other players joined me.

I got a little lucky, the flop actually fit that hand pretty well—A♣ K♠ 5♥. Gutshot straight draws to the nuts on both ends and the nut low draw, plus a backdoor heart flush draw. In Omaha, it's important to be drawing to a nut flush—second-best flushes are frequent and expensive. Though still important, it's not quite as important to be drawing to the nut flush with backdoor draws. This was about as good a flop as this hand could get. It was a good enough draw I thought it was worth a bet. Four of them liked the flop well enough to call.

The turn brought my low in, 8♦. I had half the pot and gutshot draws on both ends for the other half. I bet again, lost one player, and three of them called.

The river was a disaster for me: 3♣, counterfeiting my low. I checked and folded to a bet. A 64 won the low and a pair of Aces took the high.

This hand didn't work out for me at all—I include it because I think it serves as an example of why it's important to start with hands that have very strong draw possibilities. The possibilities of hands like this are just too weak, and the hand has no backup, no counterfeit protection. Essentially, you have to get lucky three times with such a hand. First, you have to get lucky and hit a solid flop, then get lucky and make your draw, and finally get lucky and have anyone with a better draw miss. This is a little too much to ask.

Fold This Hand

One of the worst starts in Omaha hi/lo split is a hand like 5♦ 6♠ 7♥ 9♣. At initial glance it's deceptive, looking like it has lots of straight possibilities. But, of course, any straights it makes will likely have enough low cards on board so that you'll get half the pot at best, or if the board is high cards you might make a second-best straight with the 7♥ 9♣. I was recently dealt this hand. I folded it, but the progress of the board gives an interesting illustration of how this kind of middle-card straight can go bad.

The flop was 4♣ 6♣ 8♥. I would have flopped the nuts for the high half. But it wasn't destined to stay the nuts. The turn brought the A♣ for a flush. If that wasn't enough, the river brought a 7♦, making a higher straight likely.

The high end was won by a 10 high straight.

Marginal starts give marginal results. In games where draws matter—razz, hi/lo split games, and loose hold'em games—make sure you get off to a solid start.

A Straight with Backup

Of course, sometimes you can start with a marginal draw and get lucky. I was playing Omaha hi/lo split recently and did just that. I was distracted and wasn't really paying attention when I called from midposition with 6♦ 7♣ 8♥ 9♥. This was a terrible hand. It had no flush possibilities, and the only straights it could make would either have to split the pot with a low hand or be the idiot end of a bigger straight. It was a terrible call. But I got lucky and the flop came down like manna from the heavens, 5♠ 7♦ 9♦.

Top two pair, nut straight, and there was a chance that I wouldn't have to split with a low. Of course, somebody had a flush draw, so it wasn't a perfect flop, but it certainly could have been worse.

I didn't play this hand particularly well. I shouldn't have seen the flop with the hand. But once the flop hit, it serves as a good example of having the nuts with a redraw. I guess a rainbow flop of the same ranks would have been an improvement, but generally it's hard to improve on a nut straight and top two pair.

It was checked to me on the flop, I bet and got one caller. The turn was a scare card for me, the K♦. But it was apparently a scare card for my lone opponent also, because he checked and folded to my bet. So, this is not to say you can't win with those kinds of hands. But things have to work out near perfectly for you to win. The game's tough enough without handicapping yourself.

MARGINAL DRAWS

A marginal draw is a hand that has to hit the flop to be good but doesn't have a lot of ways to hit the flop hard. An example is Q♣ 8♣. The 8 kind of drags the hand down, making it very unlikely that it will flop a solid draw like a flush draw and two overcards. Any straight the hand might make will be weak, and there will always be better straights possible. Even a hand like Q♣ 10♣, not one of the all-time great hands, is a much, much better holding.

I was recently in a hand where my opponent held a Q♣ 8♣ and I think it illustrates the kind of trouble a hand like this can get you in.

It was a short-handed game, only six of us, and I was dealt pocket 6s in late position. I raised and both blinds called.

I didn't like the flop, 9♣ 4♥ J♥, but both blinds checked, so I bet. One folded. The caller had Q♣ 8♣. He had a gutshot straight draw, an overcard, and a backdoor flush draw. Add all those marginal draws up and he did have enough of a hand to call with. That was part of his problem. He did have enough to call with, but there is nothing strong about any of his draws.

His hand improved some when the turn put 7♣ on the board. Now he had a flush draw to go with his gutshot straight draw. Again he checked. I bet. He called.

On the flop, I thought I probably had the best hand. But after he called on the turn, I wasn't so sure. In fact, I was convinced I didn't have the best hand. I was done with the hand after he called the turn. I wasn't going to bet the river unless I caught a 6. The river was K♥. We both checked and my pair of 6s held up. I was surprised to win that pot.

The lesson here is that his hand had some marginal draws on the flop and he probably did the right thing with his check/call. But when he picked up the flush draw on the turn, his hand got a lot better. Any club makes him a flush, a 10 makes him a straight, and a Queen makes him top pair. That's fifteen river cards that he can catch and have a pretty good hand. As it turns out, he could just pair his 8 and win. I think his hand was improved enough on the turn that he should have bet the hand. A bet would have won it for him right then. I think part of the reason he didn't bet was that he recognized the marginality of the hand from the get-go and his mind-set stayed at that marginal setting even when things improved a lot for him.

His problem started when he began to play the hand. He could have played the hand strongly if he'd flopped a strong draw. But that just wasn't likely to happen with a weak start.

How Often You'll Like the Flop

Most of the time you're not going to like the flop. You'll flop a pair about one-third of the time. Add in the times you'll flop a flush draw, a straight draw, or some mix of draws and you still won't like the flop over half the time.

Overcards

By itself, an overcard draw isn't much of a draw. Something like K♣ Q♣ with a flop of 9♠ 7♦ 4♦ is pretty much worthless against a loose field. Even if the turn pairs you, there's the worry that someone has K9 or Q7.

Premium overcards, such as A♠ K♠, against a small field are a good holding against such a flop, but this is partly because of the chance that the A♠ K♠ is the best hand. Against a field of three or four opponents, it's very unlikely that two overcards is the best hand on the flop. At most, you have six outs and you may be drawing dead.

Overplaying Overcards. For some reason, many players seem to think having two overcards to the flop is a good hand. I'm not sure why they think this.

I was in a recent five-handed game where I was in the small blind and was dealt pocket 10s, both black. There were a couple of limpers, I raised, the big blind folded, and the limpers called.

The flop was 3♦ 3♥ 4♥. I bet, there was a raise, and the last player folded. I called.

The turn was a black 8 and I bet, he raised, I called. The river was 10♥. I checked. He bet. I raised. He called. I showed my hand. He showed Ace 10 and grumbled about the "damn river card."

His problem wasn't that the river card finally gave him a hand that just cost him more money, his problem was that he thought two overcards was a hand on the flop.

Even five handed, an A♠ 10♠ is a marginal holding against an aggressive opponent. If you're going to play it, you should certainly play it for a raise preflop. Of course, in this case a preflop raise would have been reraised by me, but he still should have come in for a raise.

Daniel Nergeaua, a well-known tournament player, likes to think of the play of a hand as having a "flow"—a smooth transition from one step to the next, from one bet to the next. Looking for a flow in my play of this hand, you should be able to see a "jerkiness" to the flow. Call a raise, then bet. Call a raise, then bet. Passive, aggressive, passive again. This isn't a sequence that "flows" to a poker player. There is no simple beauty to the pattern. This lack of flow suggests I made mistakes in the play of the hand.

I might have made a mistake on the flop in not reraising. Some people think this, and the lack of flow to the action suggests it. But I think that lack of flow helped establish a deception. It served to confuse the opponent.

If he had a 4 or pocket 7s, I wanted him to think I had overcards. There was a large range of hands he could have had. Much more than just either overcards or an overpair to my 10s. His range of possible hands was larger than that. His unlikely hands (because of the preflop limp) were QQ KK AA AQ AK. The list would be too long to list the possible candidates. But I agree my play was way too jerky. I often play jerky like that. When I have a hand that I think is best, but might be drawing thin, I'll often just call a raise on the flop when an opponent could be betting a draw and then bet out on the turn. I don't three bet the flop because I don't want to go four bets with the hand, but I bet the turn because I don't want to give a free card. I don't always do that, but sometimes.

CHASING

A general principle of winning poker is to bet the best hand, letting the losers call your bets while trying to catch up. Don't chase is a classic piece of poker advice.

It's usually good advice, but sometimes it's not. Sometimes, the pot is large enough to justify chasing. Sometimes, your draw is good enough to actually be ahead even though it's not the best poker hand.

A Third Blind

When a new player comes into the game, or a player has been away from the table and missed his blinds, he's required to post an extra blind to get a hand (or wait for his turn at the big blind). Because of temporary disconnects and frequent turnover of players, this seems to happen often in online games.

This extra blind money is better, in terms of your odds, than an extra caller because it's not a voluntary call, and it's from a truly random hand, likely to be a more than normal underdog.

It's often correct to call with an otherwise marginal hand when there's an extra blind and you should raise when you're in front of the extra blind.

Such a situation recently occurred in an online game where I was dealt A♦ 6♦ on the button and a new player had posted from midposition.

Only one other player limped in addition to the player who posted, I raised. Both the blinds called along with the two already in. That's four opponents, but three of the four were defending blinds, so they figured to have weaker than normal hands.

The hand didn't work out well for me. I flopped a flush draw, 9♦ 9♣ 7♦, but the board was paired, making it somewhat dangerous for my draw. But I bet my draw when it was checked to me, three of them called.

I bet the turn of J♣ when they checked again and lost one player. One of the players check-raised me on the river card of 8♣. I folded my bluff, but he still showed his straight flush with 10♣ 7♣.

You can't win them all, but you can play a few weaker hands than normal when there are extra blinds posted.

When the Draw Is Ahead

As I pointed out earlier, sometimes the draw isn't actually chasing, it has the best chance to win. For example, K♣ Q♣ is a favorite to win against top pair with a flop of J♣ 10♥ 2♣. A flush draw, a straight draw, and two overcards is a very powerful draw, about as good as it gets.

Another example occurs in five-card draw when played with a bug (a Joker good as an Ace, or a wild card for a straight or flush). A hand of 8♣ 9♣ 10♣ Joker has twenty-four (nine clubs, three cards each of 6, 7, Jack, Queen, and three Aces) cards out of forty-seven unseen cards (after discarding the fifth card) to make a pair of Aces or better. This is a pretty good draw.

A 2 Percent Approximation

University of Texas math professor (and poker player) Charles Friedman suggests a simple method to approximate the chances of making a draw. Multiply the number of outs you have times the number of remaining cards to come, then multiply that product by 2 percent. The result is a slight overestimate of the probability of making the draw.

It's a good approximation if the product of the number of outs and the number of remaining cards is less than about 20 cards.

9

Tells and Hand Reading

Tells are physical or verbal mannerisms of other players that you can use as clues about the strength of the players' hands or of the intent of the players. It's an important tool in hand reading. Hand reading is the process of limiting the range of possible holdings of your opponent that involves analysis of tells, habits, behaviors, verbalizations, betting patterns, the way the hand has developed, your playing history with the players, and anything else that might be relevant.

Most of reading hands is about betting patterns; tells help, but you don't always need them. They can be a very important component of hand reading, but they aren't absolutely necessary to do the job in all cases. If you play online, betting patterns and player histories are about all you'll have available.

The first step in hand reading is observation. Gather all the information you can. Then you consider the question, "Why did he do that?" Whatever "that" might be: "Why did he bet?" "Why did he pause before he bet?" "Why did he check the flop then bet out quickly on the turn?" "Why did he look away from the board right before he bet?" "Why did he look back at his hole cards before he called?" Why?

Don't lock yourself into a conclusion. Think in terms of a range of possibilities, not just the most likely. As the hand progresses, use more information to narrow the range of possibilities, not to make yourself more sure of a specific holding. You're looking for some consistent indicators.

FUNDAMENTALS OF TELLS

Players will often involuntarily tell you what they are holding by their behavior. The theory of tells involves a rather simple duality: when they are acting they are lying, when they are being natural they aren't.

When a player goes out of his way to act strong, then he's weak. When he goes out of his way to act weak, then he's strong. A key element of using tells is the determination of whether a behavior is natural or an act.

Acting

When judging the meaning of a player's behavior, the first thing to determine is whether or not he's acting. A player who is putting on an act is probably trying to deceive you. Not always though. Some players do intentionally act strong when they are strong. Reading such straightforward players is mostly about the determination of whether the player is habitually just a straightforward, ABC player. Sometimes, it can be difficult to differentiate between a natural behavior and an act, but you have to make that distinction to use tells to read hands.

Many players are poor actors and it's relatively straightforward to determine whether they are putting on an act or acting naturally. If he's aware of his behavior, and he's aware that you see the behavior, then he's probably acting.

This is not always true. Sometimes, a player might be behaving as if he's strong, he's aware that you can see his behavior, but his hand is so strong that he literally doesn't care whether you call or not—he has the pot won and an extra bet doesn't matter to him.

Strong Means Weak, Weak Means Strong

The classic principle of tells is that when he's acting he's lying. A player who goes out of his way to act weak or indecisive is very likely to have a very strong hand. The reverse is less reliable, but a player who goes out of his way to appear very strong and sure of himself is probably very weak. This is less reliable because some players do go out of their way to act strong when they are strong. And some players act strong when they are strong because they don't care if you know it or not. But almost no one goes out of his way to appear weak when he really is weak. Some players behave weak naturally when they are weak, but they aren't going out of their way to do so.

The Huddle. I was proofreading this chapter between hands at a poker table when a classic tell came up. In a hold'em game, a player raised before the flop from the big blind. When he saw the flop of a Queen, a Jack, and a 10, he gave a sneer, a big exaggerated sneer, then went into a huddle to pretend he needed to decide whether to bet.

He'd gone out of his way to pretend he didn't like the flop and didn't know what to do. I thought he'd flopped a straight. It was only two pair.

Acting Natural Before the Huddle. A situation came up recently in a seven-card stud game where a player gave off opposite tells in two different betting rounds that were consistent even though different. On fourth street, I had a big split pair of 10s and bet into his 8♣ 7♣ board. He immediately raised and did so with an exaggerated strong flip of his wrist, throwing the chips into the pot. Such an intentional show of force often indicates weakness, an application of the strong means weak rule. It's not 100 percent reliable, but I took it to mean he probably had a flush draw. I called. I wasn't sure enough about the tell to reraise, and even if the tell was 100 percent accurate, my pair was only a small favorite against a good draw on fourth street.

Fifth street brought him a Q♣. He was high, so he acted first. He went into a big Hollywood hem and haw, looking back at his hole cards and going out of his way to suggest indecision. Finally he bet. Now, I was sure he had a flush draw and just made his flush. I folded. He winced and showed me his flush.

READING HANDS

Sometimes, you can put a player on a hand by what he doesn't do.

I was playing hold'em and had A♣ 5♥. Not what you'd normally consider much of a hand.

The player under the gun limped, just called the blind. Everybody folded to the button who raised and the small blind called. Now it was my turn.

With only the information I've given you my hand seemed like a clear fold. But I knew something about all three of these players. I had played with them for a while that evening.

The under the gun player sometimes got a little tricky, but mostly he was hyperaggressive. I didn't think he would limp with a big hand, so I didn't worry that he had a better Ace than mine. He almost certainly had some kind of middle cards, and probably not a pair.

The player on the button was on tilt. He'd been playing a while and, after an initial rush, he'd been bleeding chips, playing progressively worse, to the point where he was no longer bleeding chips, but spewing them. As time progressed, he made more and more wild raises and desperate, hopeless bluffs.

The player on the small blind was a tough, aggressive player. He also knew the same thing I did about the other two players. He wasn't going to call with a big Ace in this situation, he was going to make it three bets or fold. I knew him, and I was sure of that. If he had an Ace that he thought was too weak to reraise, then he'd fold it.

So I called the raise. My hand still wasn't all that great, but because I knew the habits and status of these players, I knew that if I did flop an Ace I'd probably have the best hand and didn't have to worry that someone else had an Ace with a better kicker.

I completely missed the flop, checked, and folded when it was a bet and a raise back to me, but this isn't the point. Knowing these players, then acting on it gave me a small edge. It didn't work out, but if you take advantage of enough of these small edges, you'll have enough of them work out to make it well worth paying attention.

Reading Hands in Low-Limit Games

A lot of people seem to think that you can't read hands in low-limit games. This line of thinking comes from the idea that low-limit players don't know whether they have a good hand or not, so they can't telegraph their hand strength. Of course, this is nonsense. Many low-limit poker players are pretty good players. Of course, every once in a while you'll run across a player who doesn't have a clue, but that's not the norm.

If you find yourself unable to read hands at all in a typical low-limit game, look to yourself for the reason, not the other players.

It can get tough if you have a player who calls all bets 100 percent of the time and never raises. Or one who always raises/reraises and never calls. But you don't really run into such extremes often. When you do, it really doesn't matter that you can't read them. They're going to lose all their money anyway.

But if a player plays every hand and sometimes he raises and sometimes he doesn't, then probably there is some kind of pattern to when he raises and when he doesn't. Maybe it's not easy to discern, but it's there.

You need to do a couple of things to get a strong read on a player. First, don't focus on yourself, focus on the other player. This is harder to do than most players think. Whether you've played for ten hours or ten minutes has pretty much nothing to do with reading other players' hands. What do you know about them? If you don't understand what I just said, you need to stop until you do.

Then, you need to focus on some particular hand—you want to read a hand, not read many hands. After that, the rest is easy.

Of course, you can't expect to be exact in your reads. But you should be able to put a player on a range of hands.

One mistake many players make when tracking others' play is to track what hands opponents will play from what position. This can be helpful in reading hands, but it's much more important how they play certain hands, not what positions they might play them from. Players will more often mix up the hands they'll play from early position for deceptive reasons rather than mix up how they'll play the hand. You need to focus more on how they play than on what particular two cards they do or don't play.

When They Bet in Hold'em

When reading hands, you start with putting a player on a range of likely hands. Then you use all the information available to you to cull that list of likely hands down.

Generally, the first thing to think when a player bets is top pair. But you also have to consider other possibilities. You need to think of more than just his hand, you need to look at the texture of the flop. With a rainbow flop of Q♥ 7♦ 2♣, an early position limper who bets out is likely to have a Queen. But the same bet from a blind hand could just as easily be from a 7.

A bet into a flop of Q♣ 9♣ 2♥ could just as easily be from a straight draw or a flush draw.

INDUCING A TELL

Sometimes, you can induce a player to give you a tell. One of the more reliable tells is when a player is noticeably trying to keep from giving off tells—an exaggerated poker face if you will.

Asking Him What He Has

I recently used a tell. It was a pretty big pot and I'd missed a draw. It was seven-card stud and I had a pair of treys. A player bet and everybody else folded. I asked him, "I haven't seen you bluff all night, can you beat a pair?" He immediately sucked in his breath and went completely rigid. He was able to say "yes" almost without moving his lips. I called. He had no pair

When a player artificially freezes, making no movement or sound, it's a strong indication that he is weak. Be careful with this one though, because some players do this when they are strong. Most players are more afraid to give away weakness than strength, but there are exceptions.

Players who are bluffing tend to be hesitant to do or say anything because of a fear that they'll give away their weakness by their actions or the tone of their voice. They are afraid of a call. Players who aren't bluffing don't have the same fear that you'll fold. They still win the pot if you fold, so that one extra bet isn't as important to them. They don't fear the risk of giving away their hand by talking because it won't cost them the pot; at most, it will cost them a bet.

If They're Unsure, Let Them Know

I tend to be pretty aggressive, and at times even somewhat animated. I sometimes just put on a show when I'm playing poker. Some people like to watch me play when I'm displaying my maniac animation.

I can think of more than a couple of people I've played with over the years who would bet just to see what I would do. They would be very uncertain about my holding and would bet as a test of my hand.

When I was unsure about calling, they would then realize that their hand was best. So at that point, the hand was over to them. They'd figured out the puzzle and didn't really care what happened next (my hand being the puzzle). Once that was done, they just didn't care whether I called or not. They'd show me their hand to prove to me that they'd figured it out, that they knew they were best.

This is the kind of situation where you can table your hand and ask, "Should I call?"

Poker is a game. People play it as a game. You'll win a lot more money letting people play the game they want to play rather than trying to force them to play the game you want them to play.

STRAIGHTFORWARD PLAYERS

Showing a Card

This is a book about casino poker. Some forms of table talk tend to be frowned on more often in casinos than in home games. But if you can get them to say something, they'll give off clues. Of course, in my case I sometimes misinterpret the clues.

We're in a nine-handed, fairly loose hold'em game. Two blinds, 50/$1, $1 to go. I have plenty of chips and a Q♥ 4♥ in middle position. I open for $2. Two players after me call, the big blind calls. The flop is Q♦ 10♥ 9♦.

The first player checks, I bet, the two players behind me fold, and the player in front of me calls. The turn is Q♣. He checks to me and I bet, he check-raises.

I hem and haw for a second, then show him my Queen, saying, "What the hell am I supposed to do, I've got a Queen but I don't think it's any good." He doesn't say anything.

I say, "I'm worried I'm drawing dead. I don't want to call if I'm drawing dead. Do I have any outs?"

He says, "A few." Then, after some silence, he says, "I have a straight draw."

I say, "You have a Queen and straight draw? So I have outs?"

He says, "You have some outs."

I call, catch a 4, and my Q♥ 4♥ beats his Q♠ J♠.

It turns out that it wasn't a very good call. I'll tell you why I called. I wasn't sure he had a Queen. I thought he did, but he could have had a J10 or even JJ instead.

The reason is that he never actually said he had a Queen. He implied it, but that's all. He did say he had a straight draw. Most players are telling the truth when they say something precise like "I have a straight draw," but not when they say something vague.

Anyway, it turned out I got lucky.

Capitalizing on Habits of Straightforward Players

I was recently in a fairly aggressive hold'em game where I was on the big blind with 3♦ 5♥. That's not much of a hand, but everyone folded except a player just to the right of the button—he limped in without a raise.

The flop was K♠ Q♥ J♣. I checked. He bet.

Now, what did he have? I didn't know a lot about this player, but he seemed to be fairly straightforward and not terribly passive. He was in a perfect position before the flop to raise and steal the blinds, but he didn't do that. That's passive behavior from a player who isn't real passive. With a big hand, a raise would have made sense because a raise would just look like a steal and probably wouldn't scare anyone away. With a couple of big cards, I'd have expected him to raise with as little as an Ace or a King. But he didn't raise, he just limped in. I concluded he probably didn't have any big cards.

I thought the flop didn't hit him very well. Maybe he had a jack, or maybe he had a 10 and flopped a straight draw, but I didn't think he had a strong hand. I didn't have anything at all. But more importantly, I didn't think he had anything either. Possibly a draw. Possibly bottom pair. Probably nothing.

I raised. He called. The turn card was 4♣. I bet. He called. The river was 2♦. I bet. He folded.

This is an example of hand reading. He limped from late position preflop. There was no way I believed he hit part of that flop. He was aggressive enough so that I think he would have raised rather than limped if he'd had a big card. And, I think he was also aggressive enough so that he would take a stab at it after I checked the flop even if he'd missed. I was a little worried when he called the turn though. He probably hit some part of that flop, he just didn't hit it very hard.

It could be I just got real lucky on that hand. The point isn't whether my read was right or wrong, but that sometimes you can be confident enough about your opponent's hand that it doesn't even matter what your own hand is.

A Straightforward Tell

I recently played with a very straightforward guy in a seven-card stud game. He would stare you down when betting trips and look downward and away from you when betting a small two pair. Once I observed that, he was an open book.

SOME COMMON TELLS

Chip Tells

There are a lot of tells related to a player's relationship with his chips. Probably the best-known chip tell is a player making a glance at his chips when he catches a card on the flop that greatly improves his hand. It's an unconscious look. A short glance, then consciously looking away.

This tell is so well known, and such a reliable tell of strength, that some tricky players will fake the tell by making a deliberate glance at their chips in an attempt to dissuade you from betting.

Other chip-related tells come from a player breaking a habit in the number of chips he grabs before it's his turn to bet. Many players don't make a move for their chips until it's their turn. When such a player does pick up enough chips to bet, call, or raise before it's his turn, it's almost a sure thing that he has a weak hand and is trying to dissuade a bet.

If a player who usually grabs enough chips to call before it's his turn suddenly doesn't touch his chips until it's his turn, then grabs enough to raise but at the last minute only calls, he probably has a fairly strong hand and really just changed his mind about raising at the last minute. This tell is sometimes faked though, so be careful with it. Like all tells, the key to reading it is determining whether it's an act or it's natural. Natural behavior isn't intended to deceive, an act is.

Protecting His Chips

You can often tell how tight a player is by looking at how he treats his stacks of chips. The idea is that a tight player tends to be physically protective of his chips, while a loose player tends to be a little more nonchalant. A tight player will keep his chips stacked nicely. A loose player will let his chips fall into unstacked piles. A tight player will use his arms to encircle his chips. A loose player will not circle his chips with his arms. A tight player will react by using his arm to block you if your hand moves close to his stacks. A loose player won't react physically. Etceteras, etceteras. These are general tendencies, not inviolate rules.

Glancing at His Cards

If a hold'em player glances back at his cards when a third flush card hits the board, then he probably doesn't have a flush. He is checking to see whether one of his big cards is the flush suit to see if he's picked up a draw.

Showing His Cards

A player who shows his hole cards to a neighbor while waiting for you to decide to call is not bluffing.

Upcards

A player who rearranges his upcards in seven-card stud to make sure that three cards to a straight flush are clearly visible, does not have a flush or a straight and at best has a draw.

TABLE TALK

Sometimes, you can pick up an amazing amount of information just by listening to what players say. This can especially be true if you're unfamiliar with the players. An example of this can be found in a situation that was described by a player posting to the newsgroup rec.gambling.poker.

At the river in an Omaha game, our hero held top two pair, Aces and Jacks, and the board showed a possible straight. That, plus the possibility that someone had a set didn't give our hero a lot of confidence in his hand. It was checked around to the button, who had been betting and raising on previous rounds. He bet and the player on our hero called. Now, even if he intended to call the bettor, when someone else had already called, the value of his hand went down. The caller wasn't bluffing, so rather than having to beat one player who might not have a hand (the bettor), he had to bet that player plus a player who he knew had a hand. The chances that he'd been beat by a straight went up considerably when the player called.

But as the player was calling, she muttered something under her breath, "Aces up is going to win this." And the call appeared reluctant, a crying call. Our hero didn't know these players. But they knew each other. The player who called seemed convinced that the bettor had Aces up. If that was true, then our hero's Aces and Jacks were good. So he called. And, yes, the bettor had a smaller Aces up.

Listen to the talk. Particularly if you don't know the players and they do know each other. You can pick up all kinds of useful tidbits.

BOOKS ON TELLS

Mike Caro wrote the bible on tells, *Caro's Book of Poker Tells: The Psychology and Body Language of Poker* (2003). This book is a must read for every serious poker player. Unfortunately, it hasn't been updated from its 1982 edition. Many of the examples in it are from draw poker, which was popular in California when the book was originally published. No matter, it discusses tells in depth and is complete with photographs illustrating the behaviors. If any book can directly and immediately translate into money won at the table, it's this book.

10

Game Selection

THE GOOD AND THE BAD

Game selection is by far the most important skill in poker. It doesn't matter how well you play if you're always picking games full of tough players. If you're a winning player, most of your winnings will come from just a handful of very bad players.

Game selection is about finding players who don't play as well as you. Avoiding players who play better than you is only a side consideration, it's not the main objective of game selection.

The Effect of Bad Players

There's no question that it pays to be the best player at the table. But do you really have to be the best, or even the second best, if the worst players at the table are bad enough?

Using Wilson Software, I did some simulations of a mediocre player with a single very good player and eight really bad players at the table.

Against the eight really bad players, the mediocre player did almost as well as the very good player. Both of them cleaned up. Replacing one of the very bad players with a second very good player showed a separation between the very good players and the mediocre player, but the mediocre player still showed a profit.

154

It takes a couple of bad players for the rest of the table to be able to beat the rake; with two very bad players and two very good players, six mediocre players can still make a profit from the leavings.

Your winnings from poker don't come from your excellent play; they come from the mistakes of others. If the other players aren't making mistakes, then you won't win.

Picking the Game

As a beginner, you probably haven't developed the self-knowledge of your own playing style or personality, so game selection can be tougher. But you can still do it. In fact, you have to do it if you want to win.

You'll want to play in loose games. This just means a lot of players who call a bet. Not only are the players in a loose game making a mistake by playing too many weak hands, but they are also playing a lot of hands that give them many opportunities to make mistakes on later betting rounds. Don't forget that your winnings come from losses of your opponents.

Until you get some experience, you probably want to avoid aggressive games. Aggressive opponents put a lot of money in the pot by frequent raises and reraises, but this means you'll also be putting a lot of money into the pot. This tends to increase your risk if you're not sure of what to do or how to react to aggression.

Nuances of preflop hand selection or playing variations on the later betting rounds can add a few dollars to your expected win. But decisions about where to sit can make the difference between whether you're an overall winner or loser.

11

Tournaments

Many players think of tournaments as a way of determining who the best player is, a way of picking champions. This belief tends to be particularly strong among those whose introduction to tournament poker came via watching the television coverage of the Travel Channel or ESPN.

But that's not really the purpose of tournaments. Tournaments are simply promotional devices of cardrooms. It is true that we call the twenty or thirty winners of various annual events of the World Series of Poker, held at Binions Horseshoe in Las Vegas every year, world champions. The World Series of Poker has over thirty events every year, and the winner of each one is crowned a world champion of something. But this is really just promotional hype.

This is not to say that the best players don't have a large edge in tournaments, that the winners of major tournaments don't tend to be good players, or that tournaments don't offer the good player an excellent opportunity for a parlay of a small buy-in to a large win. All these things are true

There's such a wide variety of tournaments these days that there is something available to suit every need. The small buy-in tournaments offered by almost every cardroom can be a lot of fun for a small, limited risk. That's the major benefit of tournaments over live play—the limit on downside risk. It can be a good way to ease yourself into playing poker for money against strangers. It's a good way to familiarize yourself with new variants of poker at a small risk. They do charge juice on these tournaments though, and sometimes the buy-in structure is somewhat deceptive, requiring rebuys to really have much of a chance at finishing in the money. But you can still get some play for your money.

TOURNAMENT STRUCTURE

The standard model for a tournament is that for a small buy-in you get a fixed number of chips. At fixed time intervals, the blinds, antes, and/or limits are increased. Doubling every thirty minutes is common. In larger tournaments, they might double every hour, in small tournaments every twenty minutes. The intent of the design of the structure is to ensure a timely completion of the event. Small events are intended to be over quickly.

Part of the buy-in is juice—money that is paid to the house as a fee and doesn't go into the prize pool. This is usually expressed as 20+5 for an event with a $25 total entry fee, $20 of it a buy-in that goes to the prize pool and $5 of it going to the cardroom as a hosting fee. In the very small tournaments, the juice can get to be pretty large as a percent of the prize money. High juice does tend to keep the better players doing something else: competing in the small buy-in tournaments. So high juice isn't all bad for the new or novice players.

Betting Structure

Most cash games in a casino cardroom are limit games with either a fixed-limit structure or the spread-limit structure common to seven-card stud. There aren't many no-limit or pot-limit cash games, and the ones that do regularly tend to have large buy-ins and blinds, are not the sort of game that a typical reader of this book is likely to jump into. I haven't talked about no-limit play in the book until now. No-limit tournaments are often offered at small buy-ins. And they do require some adjustment to the betting structure. But the basic fundamentals of tournament play don't change and for the most part I stick to those fundamentals in this chapter. What I say in this chapter is pretty much applicable to either limit or no-limit tournament betting structure.

Payout Schedule

The most important part of a tournament structure that drives strategic considerations is the payout structure. It's the payout structure that changes the strategic considerations in a tournament. In a winner-take-all tournament, strategic issues for a tournament are no different in any way than in a live game. If you get a short stack relative to the blinds in a winner-take-all event, you shouldn't play any differently than you would a short stack in a regular game (of course, in a regular game you can add chips to a short stack, but other than that a winner-take-all event is the same). The difference is that a short stack occurs more often in the tournament because of your inability to just add chips.

A graduated prize schedule, where first place gets a certain percentage, second place gets a percentage, and so on, is a different kind of game than a regular cash game. Depending on the exact situation, it can be a lot different. In a cash game, if you win all the chips you get all the money. In a tournament with a graduated payout, if you win all the chips you might get half the money, probably less than half, depending on the particular payout structure.

What this means is that one chip isn't always worth one chip. Sometimes it's worth more, sometimes less. Its actual value depends on the payout schedule and the actual chip count of every player competing in the event. It doesn't depend on just your chip count, but on how the other chips are distributed among the other players.

Generally, each chip you add to your stack is worth less than the last chip you added.

Escalation

Most of the small tournaments do allow rebuys for the first hour, so you aren't automatically busted out of the event if you lose all your chips early. Sometimes, you have to look at the fine print. Tournaments advertised as $5 events with a large guaranteed prize pool often just give you very small initial chip stacks and rebuys get you larger stacks but are much higher. Something like $5 getting you 200 chips to start with, playing initial limits of 25/50 with $20 rebuys getting you 1,000 chips isn't unheard of. I've seen tournaments where the entire initial $5 went to juice so there was no prize pool if there were no rebuys.

TOURNAMENT STRATEGY

Most tournament structures are designed to get the whole thing over with quickly. Most players think this means that they have to gamble it up right away to try to build a big stack early. As a result, you can expect about half the field to bust out quickly. This translates into a general principle that you should tend to play carefully and fairly tight in the early stages of a tournament.

But in the first hour or so of the event, you do need to be aware of opportunities to catch someone overplaying his hand. In most small tournaments, you'll find plenty of such opportunities. Other than that, you want to generally play tight in the early rounds. Just be selective about it. Don't play so tight that you pass up opportunities to add to your stack when others are offering those opportunities.

In some ways, strategy is driven by structure. But not as much as some tournament pros seem to think. Most tournament pros will refer to tournaments with slowly increasing blinds as a tournament "with a lot of play," meaning that the ratio of blinds to stack sizes starts out fairly small and rises slowly. It's that blind-to-stack ratio that drives strategy, not the speed in which the ratio rises. It doesn't really matter much whether you have a low blind-to-stack ratio because of the tournament structure or because you got lucky and tripled up the first hand. The ratio matters, but how you arrived there doesn't.

Chip Values in Tournaments

Tournament chips don't have cash value. You could almost describe a tournament outcome as an ultimate bad beat. First place gets some prize money, second place gets some, third place, and so on. Some events pay deeper than others, but a typical small tournament might play to six or ten places. The way the prize structure is set up means you have to win all the chips to get half the money. That's a bad beat.

Because of this mismatch between the proportion of the chips you win and the proportion of the money you win, chips in tournaments are more dear than real money chips. The last chip you win gives you first place money, but you would have had second place money anyway, so it isn't really worth as much as the other chips you already had—if you already had all but one chip, your chances of winning were pretty good anyway, whether or not you won the last chip right now or not. But the last chip you lose costs you everything. You're gone, busted, you have no more chance at first place, and depending on when it happens you get nothing at all.

So it works out that a chip won doesn't add as much value to your probable winnings as the value that losing a chip takes away. As such, a lot of marginal aggression should be avoided, because you don't always want to put that last bet in during a tournament.

Because of the dearness of those extra chips on your stack, you need to be more aware of the possibility of aggression from others. The value of position is heightened by the chip value mismatch. You should tend to be more careful about the hands you play from early or midposition. But at the same time, you can steal more from late position, because other players tend to be less likely to call a raise with a marginal hand. So play tighter from early position but more aggressive from late position in a tournament than you would in a regular game.

As the tournament progresses, the blinds or antes keep increasing, effectively making your stack size smaller and smaller (with respect to bet sizes). So as the tournament progresses, you have to be more and more willing to take on risk.

Taking on risk is not a bad thing. It's something you have to do to win. Most payoffs are heavily loaded toward the top end of the finishes. Finishing low in the money sometimes doesn't even return as much as your original buy-in. To get a decent win, you'll need to be among the last finishers, and this won't happen if you don't take some risks and get lucky. Just be selective in the situations you take those risks in.

Interplay of Escalation and Strategy

In the first hour or so after rebuys are no longer allowed, you can expect to lose half the field. Many of the competitors will have almost no chance to win, and once they can't buy more chips they start dropping rapidly.

Endplay

Basically, in tournaments you don't want to be caught drawing. So when the blinds/antes get big relative to your stack size, those midsized pairs become strong hands. When you have plenty of chips, playing suited cards and flopping a flush draw is a good outcome, but you'll almost never have enough chips to make that payoff. This is especially true late in the tournament.

Making a Stand. In most tournaments, the blinds are usually escalated rapidly in the later stages of the event. This means you'll often be faced with a decision to commit a large part of your stack. This is especially true if you play fairly tight in the early stages of the tournament. Often, you'll quickly reach a point where your stack is below par for the event and you simply are going to have to pick a spot to commit and make a stand. When you do reach this point, don't commit halfway. Either commit or just pass, because you need to be prepared to push all your chips in the pot.

As an example, say you're about midpoint in a no-limit tournament, have about 2,000 chips, a couple of other players have over 10,000 chips, with the average being about 4,000 chips. Blinds are

100/200. You're dealt a pair of 6s and everyone folds to you. What do you do?

You have enough chips to last for a while, so you don't have to play this hand. But should you play it? What better hand are you waiting for? You're only behind if someone has a bigger pair, and most of the field has already folded. A raise is likely to win it for you right now, and even if someone calls a raise, there's a pretty slim chance he'll have you beat without hitting a flop.

You don't really want to just call here because you don't have many chips left, and you don't want to have to be faced with a decision if you miss the flop. You don't want any callers.

What to do depends a lot on the stack sizes of the players who haven't folded yet. You don't really want a caller. The players who are most likely to call an allin bet are those with very large stacks or those with very small stacks.

So, although folding might not be a mistake, a raise is probably the best thing. But the worst thing to do here is make a small or medium-sized raise. A raise is essentially committing yourself. You don't have enough chips left to do anything but call if someone reraises, and a small raise doesn't have the power an allin raise does. An allin raise both makes it less likely you'll get another player to play with you and protects you from having to make a very tough decision on the flop.

You could limp with this hand. Or fold it. Or push it all in. But don't make a small raise. It commits you, but it doesn't give you the power a bigger raise gives you. It would just be begging a bigger stack behind you to put you all in, when he might just fold if you get it all in before his turn to act.

An exception arises if you have enough chips to make a substantial bet on the flop. When I said you don't want preflop callers, I meant that. You don't want someone with two overcards to your 6s to get to see all five board cards. If he's likely to fold if he misses the flop, then you should keep back enough chips to make a substantial bet on the flop.

The situation with something like A♣ K♣ might seem similar, but it's really a different situation. With this hand, even if you miss the flop, even if he catches up on the flop, you probably still have some outs. Putting in a small raise now, then betting at the flop even if you miss might be a good idea with this hand. In this case, even if he calls on the flop you aren't sunk, you still have a chance to win. With the 6s, if you miss the flop and bet on it, then you're probably drawing to two outs if you get called.

Deal Making and Endplay

They don't show this part on television, but many tournaments end up dividing the prize money by the final participants making a deal and chopping it up. Any player can offer a split to the remaining players, and if they all accept the deal they chop up the money. There's no requirement to chop it up; you can play on if you wish.

A lot of players like to make deals at the end because they aren't comfortable playing short handed. If this is the case, you might be better off going on and playing for the money, because their lack of confidence probably gives you something of an edge.

Heads up at the End

If down to the last two players, there are two situations: I've got the big stack or he's got the big stack. If I've got the big stack, of course I'm calling. I'm the favorite and even if I lose I get another shot. If I've got the short stack, then I probably need to get a little lucky to win—even if I'm the better player. Seeing his hand and knowing I'm a 3/2 favorite is my definition of getting a lot lucky. It doesn't do a lot of good to get lucky if you don't take advantage of it and call. In either case, it doesn't matter much if I'm a better player or not when we're heads up at the end.

GETTING LUCKY

You aren't going to win a tournament if you don't get lucky. It's a requirement for winning.

Every year about the time that the World Series of Poker starts someone starts a discussion thread on rec.gambling.poker about whether or not you should call an allin bet the first hand of the main event with AA. Sometimes, there is a variation of the thread, like should you call an allin bet if you "only" have a 60 percent edge.

The thinking of some is that if you're a good player, you shouldn't put all your chips at risk early in the event because then you can't give your "superior skill" a chance to work for you. Phil Hellmuth is the most well-known advocate of this perverse line of thinking. What's perverse about this line of thinking is that if you aren't willing to commit all your chips when you have much the best of it, then you aren't nearly as good a player as you think you are. Getting your money in the pot when you have the best of it is what being a good poker player is all about.

Let's look at a hypothetical situation that has come up for discussion on rec.gambling.poker.

Let's say at the first hand of a tournament (the World Series of Poker is usually used as an example in these kinds of discussions) you're the big blind and it's folded around to the small blind and you see his cards. He has Q♣ J♣. He pushes all his chips in. You have A♥ K♦. What do you do? You're about a 60/40 favorite in this situation.

A surprising number of people say they would fold in this situation, wanting to wait for a chance to get their money in when they have a bigger edge or to "give their skill a chance to work," whatever it is this means.

You should definitely call in this situation, no matter how much more "skillful" you think you are. A 60/40 edge is huge. You can get a bigger edge than that preflop if you want to wait for pocket Aces before you commit your stack. But the tournament will probably be over before this happens, and even if you get the Aces you can't be sure someone will call an allin bet. Can you sometimes get a bigger edge than that after the flop? Well, yes, but you can't often be sure of the edge you're getting after the flop.

A certain advantage is much more valuable than a probable one. An edge that you're sure of is a huge edge.

One way in which tournaments are different from regular games is that when you're eliminated in a tournament it's all over. There's more to figuring your odds than just looking at the odds you're getting from the chips in the pot: you have to also always be aware of the chances of going busted. Losing all your chips is a disaster.

You must accumulate chips to survive and to accumulate chips you must take risks. But you want to find ways of accumulating chips that keep your risk of going busted small. It's okay to risk chips, but risking all your chips is serious. It's important to pay attention to how the stack sizes of your opponents match up to yours. You should be more willing to take a chance and call a raise from a player with half the chips you have than to call the same raise from a player with twice the chips you have.

BLUFFING

When you move allin with a bluff, you need to be 100 percent positive your opponent will fold. Can you do that? Probably not. A bluff is very useful in no limit to steal the blinds, but when you go allin and lose, you're out. It's just way too risky. In a tournament, especially a no-limit one, you have to play tight. You have to be aggressive but still tighter than in other games.

It's very useful on the river in some cases as well. The factors that make it painful to risk also make it very hard for your opponent to call with a medium-strong hand. Sometimes, you'll get called and you're out. It depends on your opponent's stack.

SIZING UP YOUR OPPONENTS

During the early stages of the tournament, you'll see a few hyper-aggressive players. These are players who think that they have to build up a stack of chips quickly. Most of these players will bust out early. You need to quickly become aware who these players are at your table and use extra caution if they are acting behind you. If they are in front of you, use isolation raises to get heads up with them whenever you have a solid hand.

When your opponents get short stacked, you expect them to begin playing weaker hands. This starts happening in volume in the later stages of the tournament. They don't always have a lot of choice and many of them will begin to feel pressure to "do something." So the short stacks will loosen up, but the big stacks often get more aggressive whenever they're competing against a short stack.

BOOKS ON TOURNAMENTS

There really aren't any solid books on playing poker tournaments. Most of the available books are disorganized and confusing. A couple of pretty good books that will give you contrasting views on poker tournaments are *Tournament Poker for Advanced Players* (2002) by David Sklansky and *Championship No-Limit and Pot-Limit Hold'em: On the Road to the World Series of Poker* (2004) by T. J. Cloutier and Tom McEvoy.

12

Promotions

Most cardrooms run promotions other than tournaments, they have drawings, jackpots, bonuses for high hands, and other promotions. Various giveaway promotions have become the primary way poker rooms compete.

BAD BEAT JACKPOTS

The main promotion most rooms run is a bad beat jackpot. The jackpot is triggered by some specified hand, losing a pot. It might be Aces full of Queens beaten, or four of a kind beaten

Cardrooms don't make bad beat jackpots easy to hit. Various stipulations are made that serve to decrease the probability of the jackpot being beat. It's not enough that Aces full of Jacks are beaten; both hands involved must use both their hole cards to form the hand and Aces full doesn't count unless an Ace out of the hand plays. For example, (A♣ J♣) versus (A♥ Q♥) with a board of A♠ A♦ J♥ Q♣ 7♣ might trigger the jackpot but (J♣ J♥) versus (Q♥ Q♣) with a board of A♣ A♠ A♥ 7♣ 5♣ doesn't. Even though they are the same hand, Aces full of Queens beating Aces full of Jacks, in the second situation neither hand has an Ace playing from the hole cards. These rules aren't universal. Some cardrooms require Aces full beaten by four of a kind. Some require a minimum pot size or a minimum number of players dealt into the hand. The specifics vary from cardroom to cardroom, the one constant being that stipulations are made and they don't make it easy to hit.

The reason they make it difficult to hit is that a large jackpot draws players. The jackpots are progressive, so making them hard to hit serves to grow the jackpots to a large amount and keep them large.

STRAIGHT FLUSH BONUSES

Some rooms give special bonuses for a straight flush. Except for special promotions for a royal flush, such bonuses are usually during a specified time period. For example, a cardroom I play at gives a jacket for any royal flush and gives a progressive jackpot of a few hundred dollars for any straight flush from 6 P.M. to 10 P.M. four nights a week.

HIGH HAND OF THE HOUR

Some rooms pay a small bonus for the highest hand in a specified time period, per hour or per day. Often, they'll just run the promotion during off times such as during weekday graveyard shifts.

DRAWINGS

Random drawings are held at specified times. Entries to the drawings are earned by getting a certain hand, Aces full for example, or for just being in a seat when they pass out tickets.

ACES CRACKED

An Aces cracked bonus is usually for hold'em games only. If you're dealt pocket Aces, go to the river with them, and lose, then you win a prize. Sometimes, you have to go to a showdown with them or you might still be eligible if you fold and show your hand. Ask about the details.

STRATEGY CONSIDERATIONS

Bad Beat Strategic Considerations

You probably don't need to make any playing changes until the jackpot gets very large—$40,000 to $50,000 is in the large range. But when the jackpot gets large, you want to start shifting your emphasis from getting money into the pot to shooting for the jackpot. If you flop four of a kind and the jackpot is large, you want to always check/call to the river.

Straight Flush Strategic Considerations

If there is a bonus paid for a straight flush, you probably don't want to bet your draws if you have straight flush possibilities. One of the reasons for betting a draw is the possibility of winning it right there, and if you have a chance at a bonus if you hit a straight flush, then you don't want them all to fold until you've made the hand. If you make a flush, but have a draw to a straight flush, you should probably softplay your hand.

High-Hand Strategy Considerations

The only real strategy change for a high-hand promotion is you might want to take a bathroom break when it gets close to the promotion period and the current high hand isn't very high.

Strategy Considerations for Drawings

Like the considerations for high-hand bonuses, the only real consideration is to make sure you're in your seat when the drawing is scheduled or when they pass out tickets.

Aces Cracked Strategy

If the bonus for getting aces cracked is a full rack ($100) in a 4/8 game, you should probably play the Aces passively, because you'll make more if you get beat than you'll likely win in a pot.

If the bonus is smaller, like $50 in a 4/8 game, it probably isn't worth softplaying your hand. In this case, the bonus is a nice consolation prize should you get beat, but it's of marginal value compared to what you can make in a good game with pocket Aces. If the game isn't that good, then even $50 might be enough to call for softplaying your pair.

FUNDING PROMOTIONS

In most cardrooms, the promotions are funded by a jackpot rake. When each pot reaches a specified size (something like $10 or $15), $1 is taken for the pot and put into a special promotional account that promotional payouts are made from.

An example split of the jackpot rake is 40 percent to the main jackpot, 20 percent to a backup jackpot, 10 percent to a secondary backup, and 30 percent to a general promotional fund.

The general promotional fund is used for straight flush giveaways, football pools, added money in tournaments, high-hand bonuses, drawings for cash, and so on. The cardrooms make the claim that the jackpot drop is returned to the players, and in some sense they're right about that. But it doesn't really all get returned, because one of the management objectives is to grow the size of the discretionary fund overtime. This gives them more discretion over future promotions. And the moneys that are returned to the players are returned in ways to benefit the cardroom, not the players. But jackpot-funded promotions are here to stay, whether I like them or not.

THOUGHTS ON PROMOTIONS

If given the choice, and everything else is equal, I'd much rather play in a room that had no promotions and didn't take a jackpot drop. That $1 every hand adds up and is a real drain on the game.

But you'll seldom have a choice, and when you do you'll find not everything is equal. Weak players tend to gravitate to the promotions. The room that rakes more, but gives more promotions, is going to be the one with the better games.

So, even though I'd prefer a smaller rake than to have all the promotions, I follow the promotions because that's where the dead money is.

Many cardrooms maintain mailing lists and periodically will mail out coupons for promotions that are only good for patrons on the mailing list. Even if you're not sure you'll ever be back, get on the mailing list.

There are two poker rooms very near my house. Since I'm aversive to cigarette smoke, I play in the no-smoking room. But I'm on the mailing list for the other room.

A couple of months ago I got a set of coupons in the mail, one for each week of the month, for $30 in chips for a $20 buy-in to the $1 to $5 seven-card stud game. They were also having a seven-card stud promotion, where if you had the low card bring-in five times in a row you won $100. After two hours of play, they'd give you a food comp worth $10. And the restaurant was running a weekday lunch special for $4.99. For two hours of play, I got $10, plus lunch for two, plus whatever I won, plus a free roll for the $100 bonus. That's a pretty nice deal. It's not a lot, but it was a good enough deal for me to go play for two hours a week during that promotion. Every little bit helps.

13

Conclusion

If you read *Card Player* magazine, you'll often see articles on poker that compare different variations of the game by a focus on the differences between the games. I don't like this approach because I don't think it helps advance you as a poker player. The different variations all have strong similarities—they're all poker. I think that a focus on the similarities of the different variations helps develop your skills by building on strengths—it helps you learn to use the skills you already have to master new situations. Don't let anyone fool you into thinking the skills you need to play hold'em well are different from the skills you need to play seven-card stud well.

For example, hold'em is sometimes described as a game of hand domination, while seven-card stud is described as a game of live cards. Most writers present these concepts as if they're different things. But they're both ideas with an aim to avoid drawing thin. That's all. There's no difference in the fundamentals of the ideas. There may be a difference in how you implement the idea in the different game variations, but the idea itself is a constant and applies broadly among all forms of poker. Don't draw thin. That's an important poker concept whether you're playing hold'em, seven-card stud, or deuces wild spit-in-the-ocean.

LIVE CARDS AND DOMINATION

The need for live cards is usually thought of as a different concept than domination. But the two are actually closely related, both stemming from the goal of ensuring that you have ways to improve, just in case you aren't already best.

The concept of live cards is usually applied to seven-card stud or other games with private exposed cards. The concept of domination is usually applied to hold'em or other games with common or shared exposed cards.

Live Cards

When you are drawing you need to have cards to draw. Hence the concept of live cards. A live hand in seven-card stud is a hand whose cards that will improve the hand haven't already been dealt to another player. Even if you already have the best hand, you want to have redraws in case the other players catch up with you. This is why you prefer to start with low draws in seven-card stud hi/lo split. With a low draw, if you make your hand you probably will have a redraw for the high half. Or if you miss your draw, you might still back into a high hand.

Domination

In hold'em, a dominated hand is one that's currently beat and has three or fewer outs. This is the opposite of a live hand in the sense that a live hand has a lot of cards it can catch to improve but a dominated hand doesn't. Dominated hands are to be avoided.

Suited cards aren't dominated. Being suited adds a lot to a hand, often enough to compensate for the potential of kicker problems. It adds to the value in ways that are important even if you don't make a flush. It makes the hand live, giving it outs other than its pair outs.

WAITING FOR THE NUTS

I have a friend who plays a lot of low-limit hold'em and he plays tight, very tight. He wins at the game, but his average win rate is about one-third of what mine is in the same games. He wins a high percentage of the hands he contests, but he just doesn't play many hands and the pots he wins tend to be very small.

He's happy with his results, but he'd do a lot better if he'd open up a little and not always wait for the nuts before he gets aggressive.

In his very good book on low-limit hold'em, *Winning Low-Limit Hold'em* (2000), Lee Jones suggests getting rid of middle or bottom pair on the flop. He claims it won't hold up when there are a lot of players in the hand and that the hand is an overall loser.

Well, it's an overall loser if you play it indiscriminantly. But it would also be wrong to fold it indiscriminantly. Against a bet you might want to fold. But otherwise there's a good chance you're best if you have a good kicker against loose opponents. In this case, you'll probably get called by worse hands if you bet.

Jack, 5

Sometimes, players are afraid to bet or raise because they are afraid of the nuts. A recent example of why suited cards aren't dominated is a J♥ 5♥ I was recently dealt in the small blind. We were short handed and had six players. Two players limped, I called, and the big blind checked. The flop gave me a flush draw, 9♣ 3♥ K♥. I bet and got one caller. The turn was a 10♦, giving me a gutshot straight draw to go with my flush draw. So I bet again and was called. The river was the Q♥, giving me a flush and anyone with a Jack a straight. I bet, was raised, I reraised, and the player with a Jack, 10 called.

I got lucky and made the flush. I got lucky twice because the card that made my flush made him a second-best hand. But the size of the pot came from having the draw. I bet the draw and if we'd both missed on the river I might have won the pot with a bet on the river, not with the best hand. Suitedness adds strength to the hand by making it bettable. Betting a hand accomplishes a lot of things. For example, it puts the opponent in a mind-set of expectation of loss. This is why I think I'd have won it with a bet on the river if we'd both missed. He was expecting to lose because it's doubtful he'd have thought his second pair was any good.

ACTION AND THOUGHT

Poker is a thinking game. The rewards will go to the player who can outthink the others.

In the first paragraph of this book, I said action is driven by thought. I think this is true. But social psychologists tell us that it's also true that thought is driven by action. Whenever you do something, your mind will construct a story to explain the action. Bet often enough and your mind will become convinced that you're a tough, winning player who dominates others. Try it. It works.

TIPPING

My dealer friends have all asked me to include something about tipping. You aren't required to, but you are expected to tip the dealer when you win a pot. Dealers are paid minimum wage and rely on tips for the majority of their income. If you think the dealer is doing a good job, then throw him fifty cents or $1 when you win a pot. If you don't think he's doing a good job, then it's okay to stiff him.

If you win a tournament, you're expected to tip for everybody. Leave 1 to 10 percent with the tournament director and it will be split up among the dealers.

RANKING HANDS

For some reason, poker players have some sort of compulsion to try to rank starting hands in poker. Hand x is better than hand y.

Well, you can't really do that. The value of a hand depends on a lot of things, some of which aren't related to the hand itself. Just as an example, the number of players is an important variable. According to some statistics that Will Hyde calculated and posted on the internet, with two players in hold'em, a pair of 7s is the tenth best hand. But with ten players it's forty-seventh. This is because against just one opponent a pair of 7s will usually win unimproved. But with nine opponents somebody is going to make a bigger pair than 7s.

Don't try to memorize some list of "playable hands." Work on thinking about the totality of the situation and how each variable interacts with your hand to give it value.

14

An Afterthought—Patience

One thing I haven't stressed as much as I could in this book is how much patience it takes to play poker well. You have to wait and wait until a situation where you have the best of it arises and then pounce on it. But sometimes you'll wait for hours for the right situation, then things don't work out as planned and, even though you have the best of it, you don't prevail. It can be hard to go back into the waiting mode when this happens, but this is what you have to do.

THE LONG RUN

Everything evens out in the long run. There are two things wrong with this statement. First of all, the long run is a very long time—it is in fact forever. It's an infinite length of time. You never get there, you just get closer and closer. But also, everything doesn't really even out.

The reality isn't just that nothing evens out, it's that the long run is a very long time. In the 1930s, the British economist John Maynard Keynes argued that governments must combat the worldwide depression by spending money they didn't have. That went against the conventional wisdom of the time. Contemporary economists of the time argued that government intervention wasn't needed, that in the long run the invisible hand of Adam Smith would make any corrections needed to bring the economy back. Keynes's response

177

was, "In the long run we're all dead." The long run is a very long time indeed.

The Law of Large Numbers

The law of large numbers says that as an observed sample gets bigger and bigger, the sample average gets closer and closer to the theoretical average. It says that if you flip a coin enough times the percentage of heads will get arbitrarily close to half, no matter how many times it comes up tails the first few flips. If the first 10,000 flips are all tails, you'll still average 50 percent heads if you just keep flipping it long enough.

This does not mean that the number of tails and heads evens out. It just means that the long run is such a long time that any finite discrepencies between heads and tails are insignificant. Even though the difference becomes arbitrarily small, they won't balance each other out. Luck does not even up in the long run.

THE GAMBLER'S FALLACY

The gambler's fallacy is the belief that everything eventually evens out. Roulette systems that say bet black after red are based on it. Betting systems that increase your bet after a loss are based on it.

It's wrong. Things don't even out. What's done is done and the future is independent of the past. It takes a long time for things to look like they've evened out. But things only start to look like they've evened out because if you go at it long enough the time itself dominates the results and individual results just aren't noticeable. They don't even out, you just don't notice them anymore.

RANDOMNESS

To illustrate what can happen, and how long you have to wait at times, I ran a number of simulations with Texas Turbo Hold'em (available from wilsonsoftware.com). This poker simulation package allows you to specify playing habits of players and put together a table of players with characteristics you specify. I simulated a $10/20 game, with $3 rake and our hero in the simulation toked $1 when he won a pot. I set up the opponents so that our hero was a winning player (in a raked game no one will be a winning player unless the opponents are making a lot of mistakes). On average (based on a 7 million hand simulation), our hero was slightly less than a $10 per hour winner (assuming thirty-five hands per hour). This is smaller than the one big bet an hour that is generally accepted to be an acheivable win rate, but it's probably closer to what most of you will experience.

I then simulated a sequence of five-hour playing sessions. In the first fifty trials I ran, our hero lost money in half of them. Half. And his win rate was slightly higher than his overall average—he won $10.77 per hour. A winning poker player—and he loses half the time. This can get real discouraging.

The reason he was an overall winner even though he lost half of the sessions is that his winning sessions tended to be bigger than his losing sessions. The range was a high of +$816 and a low of -$615. Twelve sessions gave wins over $300 and only five sessions had losses worse than -$300. A few large wins compensate for many small losses. This is typical of what you'll experince at the table if you play in loose games.

To carry the example forward a little, I did a second simulation of fifty five-hour sessions. Twenty-six (52 percent) of them involved a losing session for our winning poker player. But he was still a winner, at a rate of $9.77 per hour this time. The range of his session results was a high of $1,310 and a low of -$822, again a wide range, skewed to the positive side.

For the first 100 sessions I simulated (five-hour sessions), our hero averaged $10.27 per hour, $51.34 per session. Separating the winning sessions from the losing ones, his average winning session win was $356.73 and his average losing session loss was -$254.04.

Don't get the idea from this that your result will always end up close to your long-run expected value. Far from it. At times, you'll have major deviations from the long-run average, sometimes deviations that will last a long time.

The next simulation I ran demonstrates this. Assuming five-hour playing days, five days a week, fifty weeks a year, I simulated day-by-day play for a year, which totalled to 250 five-hour sessions. Note that for all but the first few days our hero was in the red. He quickly got into the red and stayed there for the rest of the year. A seventeen-day losing streak started on day eight and by the end of the year our hero had still not recovered.

This isn't a typical result for a winning player but it isn't as rare as most players think. I didn't run a bunch of sims and pick out one to illustrate this point. This point was illustrated all by itself.

A true appreciation of randomness isn't really a normal human trait. The gambler's fallacy somehow just seems right to humans, even to those who know better. It just seems right, but it's not right.

People persist in believing that if you spin a roulette wheel for an infinite amount of time all numbers will be picked an equal number of times. But this is just not right. All numbers will occur an equal proportion of times. The number of times will diverge. It might seem like a nit to make this distinction, but it really is an important distinction.

I recently read *Randomness* (1998) by Deborah J. Bennett, in which she talks about why it took so long for scientific ideas of probability to develop in the history of ideas. She argues that one reason is that humans just have a hard time accepting the idea that sometimes things just happen, that there doesn't have to be a reason. This is how religion developed, "God made that tree limb fall on his head."

IT'S NOT MY FAULT

This difficulty in really accepting randomness seems to be a normal human trait. Another typical human trait that contributes to this is what psychologists call attribution error. You see this one in poker players all the time: if you win, it's because you're good at it, if you lose, it's bad luck. You attribute success to internal causes (your personal skills) and attribute failure to external causes (bad luck).

Phil Helmuth, a well-known tournament player and author of a popular book on poker, is one of the worst in frequent demonstrations of the attribution error at work. An example is a hand that busted him out of a recent tournament. In a no-limit hold'em game, he had a pair of Queens against his opponent's pocket pair of Jacks before the flop. All the money went in the pot before the flop. A Jack came on the river, beating Phil's pair of Queens with three Jacks. Phil threw his usual fit, moaning about what bad luck he'd had. Of course it was bad luck to have the pair of Queens beat by a pair of Jacks—before the flop Phil was better than a four to one favorite. But while bemoaning that particular bad luck, Phil forgot how lucky he had been in the first place to have been dealt Queens at the same time an opponent had Jacks. For him to have been in the situation where he was a big favorite, he first had to get lucky.

What happens with Phil, I think, is that he makes the normal attribution error: when he wins he crows, when he loses he thinks the cause is something outside of himself. But since he doesn't really internalize ideas of chance and randomness that external cause can't just be happenstance, he has to put a face on it—it's got to be the other guy. I don't mean to be picking on Phil, he's just the best-known example of attribution error in poker. We all do it to some extent.

I think many poker players suffer from this. They want there to be a reason for everything. They know probability, and they know odds, but in their gut they don't accept it. There has to be a reason. This could have been avoided if someone hadn't screwed up.

I think Phil falls into this catogory. He knows the odds. But deep in his gut he doesn't accept the idea that things just happen, that things can really be random.

And it takes a very long time for this randomness to start to look stable.

Appendix: Public Cardrooms

(Note: Most of this material appeared in my previous book, *The Complete Book of Hold 'Em Poker)*

INITIAL VIEW OF THE ROOM

When you walk into a large cardroom for the first time, it can look chaotic at the initial glance. The noise and the people can be disorienting at first. Relax, it'll soon just be part of the scenery for you.

Most rooms have a railing that separates the playing area from the waiting area of the cardroom. It's often a good idea to spend a few minutes standing at the rail, just getting an overview of the room. Don't stand right next to a table unless the rail is separating you from it and don't stand directly behind a player. It bothers some players.

The particular procedures involved in getting into a game are not standardized—they vary from room to room. The specifics will depend on the room. Don't hesitate to ask a cardroom employee if you are unsure of a procedure.

SIGN-UP PROCEDURES

Somewhere in the room will be a floor manager or host, usually called the "brush" in a poker room. Before you can take a seat at a table, you'll have to find him. He maintains a sign-up sheet for the waiting list in each game.

You'll need to be prepared to tell the floorman or brush what game (hold'em) and what limit you want to play. Ask him what limits are available. Put yourself on the list for any limits you will be comfortable playing.

You can't just sit at an empty seat, just because a seat is empty doesn't mean it's available. It may be that a new player is on his way to take the seat or there may be some other reason the brush will want you to take a seat at a different table. You will not generally be allowed to take a seat without referral by the brush, so don't try.

The form of the sign-up sheet varies from cardroom to cardroom. Some use a large blackboard or acrylic writing surface and players can add themselves to the list. More commonly, someone will stand near the board and add your initials or name. Sometimes, the floor manager keeps a clipboard that contains the waiting lists.

If you see a large board that looks as if it might be a sign-up board, go to it. You should find a floor manager nearby. If you don't see such a board, look for a podium either near the front or middle of the room. If all else fails, just ask someone where to sign up for a game.

Whenever you're in doubt about something, don't hesitate to just ask whoever is available. Since every cardroom has a slightly different sign-up procedure, you won't be identifying yourself as a novice by asking. Even the most experienced player may have to ask if it's his first visit to that particular cardroom. You'll usually get a receptive reaction to questions from players and employees alike.

Once you've signed up for a game, don't leave the cardroom area without first telling the brush. Some cardrooms will give you a beeper to carry if you intend to wander to other areas of the casino.

Sometimes, they'll page you over the casino loudspeaker. Some of them are even starting to keep computerized lists shown on monitors scattered around the room. If you don't tell them you will be out of the area, many cardrooms will simply cross your name off the list if you don't quickly respond when your name is called. It all depends on the procedures in use at the particular cardroom. *Ask.*

TAKING YOUR SEAT

Once a seat is available, your name will be called out or you'll be paged. When you respond, you'll be told at which table to take a seat. Usually, the tables are numbered on signs hanging over the table that also give the game and limits and the buy-in. Sometimes, they are numbered on a small plaque, face up on the table next to the dealer.

Buying Chips

In some cardrooms, players buy chips from the dealer. In some, the brush will take your money and get chips for you from the cage. Some rooms have chip runners who carry chips around in a pouch to sell to players. If you're not sure of the procedure in your cardroom, just get out your money and someone will get you some chips. Again, you just might need to ask.

HOW TO CHANGE TABLES

Often, you'll find yourself at a table that just isn't working for you. Maybe some of the more passive players have left and have been replaced by aggressive ones. Maybe vice versa. It might be time to change tables. The floorman or brush maintains two types of lists: waiting lists and change lists.

Waiting Lists

Each limit has its own waiting list. They don't maintain a waiting list for hold'em, they maintain a list for 3/6 hold'em, a separate waiting list for 10/20 hold'em, and so on. So it's a good idea to keep your name on the waiting list for all limits for which you have enough of a playing bankroll. If your name comes up on a list for a different limit than you're playing, you can just decline if you think your table has a better game. If you have your name on the waiting list for other limits, it's important to keep an eye on the other games, constantly evaluating their potential. When your name is called, you will have to move or decline, you won't be given time to watch the game for a while before you decide.

Change Lists

Changing to another table at the same limit is an entirely different procedure. When they have more than one table at the same limit, cardrooms keep a list of players who want to change tables, but the actual procedures for doing this vary widely. In some cardrooms, one of the tables is designated as a "must move" table. If table two is a must move table, then whenever a seat opens at table one, the player who has been on table two the longest must move. New players are always seated at table two. If the cardroom you play at designates must move tables, then you'll probably have to negotiate something with the other players if you want to move before your turn.

In cardrooms that don't designate must move tables, changing to another table at the same limit is still not a standardized procedure. Some rooms keep a formal change list to allow players already seated in a game the option of taking a new seat when one opens up. In most cardrooms, however, the brush will rely on his memory to maintain a change list. Especially if they are busy enough to have more than one table at the same limit, you can count on the brush's memory being faulty. You'll have to maintain some vigilance of your own to make sure you are allowed to move to an open seat—once a new player has been seated it'll be too late. One of the benefits of playing in large cardrooms is that there are often other tables available for a change. When you're seated at a table, always ask the brush to put your name on the change list. You should keep yourself on the list for other limits within the range you're comfortable with. Pick a good table and be prepared to change when the conditions change.

KNOW THE RULES

"A wildcat is only good once a night." That's the punch line from an old poker joke. A player goes to a draw poker card club for the first time. After a couple of hours, he gets four Aces and bets heavily. He gets called by a player who shows a hand of Q9732, four different suits. The dealer starts to push the pot to the player with the Q high hand. Our hero says, "Hey, I've got four Aces." The dealer says, "Yes, but he's got a wildcat," pointing to a sign on the wall that says, "A wildcat consists of Q9732 and is the best hand."

Well, as you might have guessed, later our hero gets a Q9732 himself and, after much betting, gets shown the sign that says, "A wildcat is only good once a night."

Although few clubs have a wildcat rule these days (although some California clubs do have some weird house rules), a novice casino player does need to realize that the house rules aren't going to be the same as the rules at home games. String betting is an example. Showing all your cards at the showdown, even when you aren't using them all to make your hand, is another. Sometimes, a violation of these rules will cost the novice a bet. Sometimes the pot.

Knowing the house rules is important. Watch, listen, and ask questions. Some rules are relatively standard and I discuss a few of them here, but there is always the possibility of a weird house rule. It pays to ask.

Protect Your Hand

Sometimes, particularly if you're in a seat adjacent to the dealer, the dealer will accidentally grab your cards and put them into the muck. If this happens, then your hand is dead. It's as if you have folded. It's your responsibility to keep control of your cards. You can't move your cards over the edge of the table, so the best thing to do is to place a chip on top of your cards whenever you leave them lying on the table. This will prevent the dealer from accidentally scooping up your cards.

Keep Your Cards on the Table

Don't pick your cards up and hold them close to your chest to look at them. Leave your cards on the table, cup your hands over them, and bend up the edges of the cards to look at them. Watch the other players to see how it's done.

The reason for this is a rule that says that no card can cross an imaginary barrier at the edge of the table. If you do move your cards behind the edge of the table, your hand can be ruled dead. Most cardrooms do not strictly enforce this rule at the low-limit tables. But you will be corrected if you do it, and if you persist in doing it, you will eventually have your hand declared dead. Just don't do it.

On a related note, should the dealer accidentally deal your card to you in such a way that it flips off the table onto the floor, do not reach down and pick it up. You are not supposed to touch any card that's off the table. The floorman will come over and pick up the card. The reason for these rules is to protect the integrity of the deck.

Show Both Cards

Your hand consists of the two cards you're initially dealt. You don't have to use both those cards to make up your poker hand, but you must have both of them to win. Show both your cards at the showdown by simply turning them face up. Do this even if only one of them is being used to form your poker hand.

One Player to a Hand

Don't ask a friend for advice at the table and don't give advice to a friend, even if one of you is not involved with the pot or if your friend isn't playing at the table. Consulting with another person about how to play a hand isn't allowed. Also, don't show your hand to another player, even if he is not involved in the pot or if you are folding.

String Bets

A string bet is a bet that's made in two motions. It's common in home games to hear a player say, "I call your dollar," put a dollar in the pot, then say, "and raise you a dollar," as he reaches into his stack of chips for a second chip. That's a string bet. In a casino, if you're going to raise simply state "raise." Don't say something like "I'll call your bet and raise you." Just say the one word, "Raise," and put all your chips into the pot at one time, not in two motions of your hand.

The reason for this rule is to reduce the chances for players to engage in what's called angle shooting. Without this rule, players can call a bet, wait to see your reaction to the call, and if you react in a way that suggests you didn't want to be called they will raise. Not allowing string bets reduces the opportunity for this kind of unethical move.

Raising

A raise must be at least the size of the bet. For example, if in a 1-4 game I bet $4 and you want to raise, you must raise by $4. If I had bet $2, then you could raise by $2, $3, or $4. You cannot make a $2 raise if the original bet was $4.

Be Careful What You Say

Verbal declarations usually count. "Call and raise" is the verbal equivalent of a string bet and, in some cardrooms, if you say this before you put your chips in the pot you will be limited to a call.

Splashing the Pot

When you make a call or bet, just place your chips in front of you. Don't toss your chips into the pot. The dealer will count your chips before putting them into the pot to ensure your bet is the correct amount. Just throwing your chips directly into the pot is called splashing the pot because of the bouncing of the chips that usually results. Don't do it. Again, the purpose of the rule is to protect you.

Act in Turn

In hold'em, the action at each betting round begins with the first player to the left of a designated dealer. Each player then acts in turn. Don't act until it's your turn—don't fold or bet early.

Table Stakes

All cardroom games are played at table stakes. This means you can't go into your pocket for more money during the play of the hand. You can't be bet out of the hand either; you will remain in competition for whatever the pot is up to the point where you've run out of chips. This is called creating a side pot. You can buy chips to add to your stack at any time between hands. You cannot add to your stack during the play of a hand.

Ratholing

Ratholing is the poker term for taking money off the table and slipping it into your pocket. It's not allowed. Except for incidental uses, such as tipping the cocktail waitress, taking money off the table is not allowed.

Short Buys

Every table has an established minimum buy-in, so your first purchase of chips must be at least that amount. At some cardrooms, after the initial purchase, it is permissible to buy less than the minimum buy. This is called a short buy. Almost all cardrooms will allow a short buy if you are not out of chips. Some will allow a short buy when you run out of chips only once.

Dealers

The dealer is an employee of the cardroom and is at work. If you have a question about the game, ask the dealer. If you want to talk about last night's football game, talk to one of the other players. The dealer's job is to keep the game running smoothly, not to provide you with a conversation.

GLOSSARY

ABC player An exceptionally straightforward player.

Allin The table stakes rule says that you can only bet up to the amount of money you had in front of you at the start of a hand. When you've bet (or called) up to that amount you're said to be allin. You've put all the money into the pot that you can for that hand. Other active players can continue to bet among themselves, but they'll compete for a side pot. You're hand will compete for the pot at the point where you where able to match all bets.

Angle An action that's not explicitly against the rules, but is considered a serious ethical violation and unfair act.

Angle shooting The use of angles to gain an unfair advantage.

Baby card A wheel card, an Ace, 2, 3, 4, or 5.

Backdoor A draw where you have three of the five cards you need on the flop. To make your hand, you need the right cards on both the turn and the river. Three cards to a flush on the flop is a backdoor flush draw.

Backraise Calling a bet, then reraising when someone raises. Sometimes called sandbagging, it's a form of slowplay.

Bad beat When a very good hand is beaten by a hand that had to make a long-shot draw, such as a backdoor draw, then it's called a bad beat.

Bet odds The odds you get from the number of callers on a bet-

191

ting round. If you bet and four players call, then your bet odds are 5-1.

Blind An initial forced bet that is put out before the cards are even dealt—a blind bet. It's used in hold'em to replace the ante in getting some initial money into the pot.

Blind, big The largest of two blinds. Usually, this blind is the same size as the bet size on the first betting round.

Blind, small The smallest of two blinds. Usually, this blind is half the size of the bet size on the first betting round.

Bluff A bet that can't win if you're called. There are generally two ways for a bet to win. One is for the opponent to fold, conceding the pot, the other is for the opponent to call and your hand prevail in a showdown. A bluff has only one way to win.

Board The community cards in the middle of the table are called the board. It consists of either three, four, or five cards, depending on the betting round.

Book player A player who plays in a rigid style. Book players tend to overvalue the concepts of patience and tend to think that hand value is determined by the cards themselves. Waiting for an obviously superior hand is their primary approach to the game.

Brush A low-level cardroom employee who acts as an assistant to the floorperson.

Burn card The card on the top of the stub that's discarded by the dealer before dealing cards for the next betting round. This is done to minimize the advantage a player would get if he caught a glimpse of the top card, knowing that the card would be dealt to the board for the next betting round.

Button The last player to act, before the blinds, is called the button. The button player is designated by a plastic disk that rotates among the players. It is used to designate the player who holds the dealer's position in the betting order.

Call When another player bets you must either call by putting an amount equal to the bet into the pot (sometimes called equalizing the pot) or fold. If you don't have enough chips to completely equalize the pot, you can go allin and call for only the chips you have.

Calling station A weak, passive player who will seldom bet or raise but will call bets with very weak hands.

Capping *See* four-betting.

Check-raise A form of slowplay. Checking with the intent of raising if another player bets.

Cold call Calling a bet and a raise all at one time. If a player in front of you bets, a second player raises, and you call, then you've cold called the raise. If a player in front of you bets, you call, someone else raises, and you call the raise, then you've called the raise, not cold called it.

Cold-decking A form of cheating where a prearranged deck is put into the game and given a false shuffle.

Dog *See* Underdog.

Dominating power hands These are hands that are very strong and should almost always be played, even in situations that mean calling a raise from an early position raiser.

Dominated power hands These are hands that are strong enough to be worth raising with from early position, but are probably not strong enough to call a raise from an early position raiser unless two or three other players have already called.

Door card In seven-card stud, your first upcard.

Drawing dead When even if your hand makes the hoped-for improvement, it can't win (e.g., the flop is all of one suit and someone has a flush and you've got a straight draw).

Drawing hand In general use, a drawing hand on the flop is one that probably has to improve to win. Before the flop, drawing hands are those two-card combinations that hope to flop a drawing hand. A hand like 7♦ 6♦ is a drawing hand. You're hoping to flop either a flush draw or a straight draw. In this book, I use the term "drawing hand" to categorize a group of hands that have sufficient chances of winning to be worth calling a raise if two or three other players are active, even though the hand is probably not best starting out.

Fancy Play Syndrome (FPS) A tendency to try to be tricky when it's unwarranted. A player with FPS bluffs too much, semi-bluffs too much, and generally plays too aggressively.

Fish A bad player who can be counted on to lose his money.

Flop In hold'em, the first three of the five community cards that make up the board. Sometimes called fifth street, because five cards have been shown to you, your two-card hand plus the three community cards.

Fold To concede any claim on the pot by discarding your hand rather than calling a bet.

Four-bet To make the last raise. Most cardrooms have a limit of one bet and three raises per round. So, the fourth bet is the third, and last, raise. Sometimes it's called capping it. To cap the betting is to four-bet it.

FPS *See* Fancy Play Syndrome.

Gambling hand A hand that does not figure to be the best hand and has long-shot chances of developing into the bets hand. These hands are usually playable preflop when six or more other players are active. You should usually not call with these hands if the hand is going to be heads up, but if seven or more players will call a raise, these hands are often worth a raise preflop when you're in late position.

Gutshot An inside straight draw. A straight draw has eight outs. This is a hand like 6789. An inside straight draw is a hand like 5689 and has only four outs.

Heads up A two-player contest. Whenever there are exactly two active hands, the hand is said to be played heads up.

Hidden pair In seven-card stud, when your two downcards consist of a pair. Sometimes called pocket pair.

Huddle A pause before acting with an indication of deep thought and concentration.

Implied odds The odds you are getting from an expectation of calls on future betting rounds.

Limp Calling the blind bet in the preflop round of betting without raising. Also, limping into a pot. If this is done as a sandbag, it's sometimes called a limp-reraise. In seven-card stud it's to just call the bring-in.

Live Used in the context of either live hand or live one.

Live hand A hand that has not been folded, where all bets have been equalized.

Live one A player who can be expected to lose chips quickly.

Kicker The highest odd card when you have a pair. If you have a pair of Aces with a King, a 10, and a 7, then you have a pair of Aces with a King kicker. It's often used to denote the lowest of the two cards in your private hand. For example, if you have an Ace and a 10, you might say you have an Ace with a 10 kicker. If your 10 pairs a 10 on the board, then you'd say you had a pair of 10s with an Ace kicker.

Kill An extra blind that doubles the limit. If the game is a 10/20 limit game with 5/10 blinds and a player puts out a $20 kill, the game becomes a 20/40 game with three blinds for that hand.

Kill blind *See* kill.

Overcall Usually refers to bets and calls as the last action, on the river. If there is a bet and a call, the second caller is called an overcall. It generally takes a stronger hand to overcall than to call because the caller isn't bluffing.

Main pot If a player goes allin, the amount of the pot that's been equalized is set aside as the main pot. Any further action by other active hands goes into a side pot that the allin player does not compete for.

Maniac A wild, very loose, very aggressive player. He plays a lot of hands and almost always raises when he plays 1, and will frequently raise on a bluff or with a very weak hand.

Morton's theorem A technical result that shows that there are certain combinations of pot odds and outs that your opponents can have that create a situation where you don't profit from a bet if they all call. They all profit from the call and the largest portion of the profit goes to the best draw.

No limit A betting structure where the only limit on bet size is the amount of chips on the table.

Nuts (also nut hand) The best possible hand. For example, if the board does not contain a pair, then an Ace high flush is the nuts.

Odds *See* bet odds, implied odds, and pot odds.

Opener The first player to voluntarily put money into the pot. The first money in the pot outside of the blinds or forced bet.

Open-raise On the first betting round, the first player to voluntarily put money into the pot can do so by either calling the blind or by raising. A raise by the first player to voluntarily put money in the pot on the first betting round is called an open-raise.

Over pair A pocket pair higher in rank than the highest card on the board.

Outs The number of cards that can be turned up on the next round that will improve your hand to a probable best hand.

Pocket Your private two-card hand in hold'em. The first two downcards in seven-card stud.

Pocket pair A pair of cards of the same rank as your private two-card hand in hold'em. In seven-card stud, a hidden pair as your two downcards is sometimes called a pocket pair.

Pot odds The odds the current pot size is giving you to make a call. It is based on the number of bets in the pot and is the ratio of the number of bets you have to call to equalize the pot and the number of bets in the pot.

Position Your order in the betting sequence. If you're one of the first players to bet, then you're in early position. If you're one of the last players to act, then you're in late position. If there are one or more players who act before you and there are one or more players who will act after you, then you are in middle position.

Preflop The first betting round. It's the betting round after you've been dealt your two-card hand, but before the flop is dealt.

Proposition player A player who is employed by a cardroom to play. He's used to start new games or to sit in on short-handed games to keep them going for a while. A prop player plays his own money and plays in the games he's assigned, but makes his own choices about how he plays. *See also* shill and stake player.

Raise You raise by putting an extra bet in the pot, requiring other active hands to either equalize the pot by calling your raise or fold.

Rake Money taken out of the pot by the house dealer. Usually between $3 and $5 per pot. Also called the cut. This is the fee the house extracts for providing the game.

Reraise A raise after a previous raise by someone else.

Reverse tell Faking a tell.

Ring game A regular game, as opposed to a tournament.

River The last card is called the river card. In hold'em, this is the fifth community card put on the board. The river betting round is the last betting round of the hand.

Rock A usually passive, very tight player.

Sandbagging A form of slowplay. Usually means calling a bet when players are left to act behind you, intending to reraise if someone in later position raises. Sandbagging on the preflop round of betting is often called a limp reraise.

Semibluff A bet with more cards to come when you probably don't have the best hand, but have outs if you're called.

Set A form of three of a kind where you have two of the rank in your hand and one on the board. Because of the community card nature of hold'em, this is a much stronger hand than three of a kind made with one card from your hand matching a pair on the board. That's because with a pair on the board, any player who has the fourth card of that rank also has three of a kind. If you have, for example, three Kings made as a set, then no other player can hold three Kings.

Shill A cardroom employee who helps start new games by sitting in with house money. He doesn't get any portion of his winnings and is not responsible for his losses. Often, he's given a set of rules to play by, generally he'll play tight and passive. *See also* proposition player and stake player.

Showdown When all the cards are out and all the bets have been equalized, the active hands show themselves to determine what the winning hand is.

Side pot Bets made after one player is allin are put in a side pot.

Slowplay Playing a strong hand in a way that suggests you have a weak hand. Sandbagging and check-raising are forms of slowplay. The term "slowplay" often refers to checking and calling on the flop, intending to bet and raise on the turn, when the bet size increases.

Slowroll On the river, waiting until everyone else involved in the showdown has turned over their cards before showing yours, even when you think you have the best hand. This is considered bad etiquette by some.

Speculative hand Speculative hands are a group of hands that don't figure to be the best hand but are getting sufficient odds for a preflop call if four to five other players are active in the pot.

Split pair When you have a pair in seven-card stud with one of the pair face up and the other face down.

Spread limit A betting structure that allows any bet size within a specified range.

Stake player A player who has a financial backer. This is very common in tournaments, where one backer will stake more than one player in return for a percentage of their winnings. *See also* proposition player and shill.

Steal-raise On the preflop round of betting, an open raise from a late position player who hopes that everyone will fold and that he will win the blinds.

Stone killer An extremely tight aggressive player.

Straddle A voluntary extra blind. But, unlike a kill, it does not raise the limits, it's just a blind raise within the nominal limits.

Structured limits A betting structure that specifies the bet size at each betting round.

Tell An involuntary action that gives observers a clue as to your holding.

Tight aggressive player A player who plays few hands, but when he does play he plays very aggressively, betting and raising often.

Tilt (going on tilt) A psychological state where you're playing very badly. The term is borrowed from pinball.

Turn The fourth card placed on the board as a community card. The betting round after the turn is usually at a bet-size double the size of the bets on the previous round. The previous round is the flop round.

Under the gun The first player to act.

Underdog An underdog has the odds against him.

Under pair A pocket pair smaller in rank than the highest card on the flop.

UTG *See* under the gun.

Value bet On the river, a bet that figures to win if called.